FROM BLUE TO RED

FROM BLUE TO RED

THE RISE OF THE GOP IN ARKANSAS

JOHN C. DAVIS

THE UNIVERSITY OF ARKANSAS PRESS
FAYETTEVILLE
2024

Copyright © 2024 by The University of Arkansas Press. All rights reserved. No part of this book should be used or reproduced in any manner without prior permission in writing from The University of Arkansas Press or as expressly permitted by law.

978-1-68226-244-3 (cloth)
978-1-61075-808-6 (electronic)

28 27 26 25 24   5 4 3 2 1

Manufactured in the United States of America

Designed by Daniel Bertalotto

∞ The paper used in this publication meets the minimum requirements of the American National Standard for Permanence of Paper for Printed Library Materials Z39.48-1984.

Library of Congress Cataloging-in-Publication Data

Names: Davis, John C., 1985– author.
Title: From blue to red : the rise of the GOP in Arkansas / John C. Davis.
Description: Fayetteville : The University of Arkansas Press, 2024. | Includes bibliographical references and index. | Summary: "Once one of the most Democratic states, Arkansas became ardently Republican in just a few years. While the dramatic shift in the partisan makeup of Arkansas officeholders may appear to have happened almost overnight, the rise of the Republican Party in the state was actually years, if not decades, in the making. From changes in voter preference at the top of the ticket in the 1960s, to generational replacement in Arkansas's political power structure in the 1990s, to a more nationalized and polarized electorate—the ascent of the Republican Party in Arkansas serves as a model for explaining partisan change throughout the country"— Provided by publisher.
Identifiers: LCCN 2023026628 (print) | LCCN 2023026629 (ebook) | ISBN 9781682262443 (cloth) | ISBN 9781610758086 (ebook)
Subjects: LCSH: Republican Party (Ark.) | Republican Party (U.S. : 1854–) | Arkansas—Politics and government—1951–
Classification: LCC JK2358.A75 D38 2024 (print) | LCC JK2358.A75 (ebook) | DDC 320.9767—dc23/eng/20230812
LC record available at https://lccn.loc.gov/2023026628
LC ebook record available at https://lccn.loc.gov/2023026629

This book would not have been possible without the collaboration and financial support of the David and Barbara Pryor Center for Arkansas Oral and Visual History at the University of Arkansas.

To Ember, John Lee, and Grace, with love

CONTENTS

Acknowledgments ix

1 —
Introduction 1

2 —
The Three Generations of the GOP in Arkansas 11

3 —
The Changing Arkansas Electorate and the Rise of the GOP in Arkansas 35

4 —
State Party Organizations and the Rise of the GOP in Arkansas 61

5 —
State Government and the Rise of the GOP in Arkansas 81

6 —
Conclusion 101

Notes 115

Index 125

ACKNOWLEDGMENTS

Were it not for the numerous contributions of those who extended to me their expertise, insight, patience, and kindness, the full scope of this book would not have been possible. A few years before I would become executive director of the David and Barbara Pryor Center for Arkansas Oral and Visual History at the University of Arkansas, the Pryor Center granted me the opportunity to lead a project exploring the topic of this book. I had considered a book-length study on the state's partisan change before being approached by the Pryor Center, but my collaboration with them no doubt made the completion of this book more tenable. The Pryor Center collaboration, which shares the same title as this book, permitted me to collect oral histories of individuals who have studied and lived through the partisan changes the state has recently undergone. We first began work in the winter of 2020. Despite the setbacks and challenges posed by the COVID-19 global pandemic, the Pryor Center afforded me the ability to conduct twenty interviews with scholars, journalists, elected officials, and activists—each of whom contributed to my understanding of the topic and aided in my conceptualization of the book. Several quotes from individuals I interviewed for the Pryor Center project are featured in this book and serve to contextualize and humanize the subject matter in ways my own words or another form of data could not. I simply cannot say enough about the brilliant team at the Pryor Center—led by their (now retired) executive director, Dr. William A. Schwab—who not only offered their technical expertise and talents but also generously supported this endeavor financially. Dr. Angie Maxwell and Dr. Janine A. Parry offered their advice on the interview project and the conceptualization of this book early on—I thank them for their feedback and guidance. I thank each person who sat down with me and contributed to the project as well as those who offered their valuable time to review the manuscript. Before this manuscript was fully developed, Drs. John C. Green, David B. Cohen, and Kenneth M. Miller graciously accepted an early, condensed version of this study as a chapter in their co-edited volume *State of the Parties 2022: The Changing Role of American Political Parties*. Their feedback and support improved the overall project. I wish to thank the University of Arkansas Press, especially Mike Bieker and David Scott Cunningham, for their confidence in my ability to see this project through. Also, I must recognize and thank the managing editor for the press, Janet Foxman, for her thoughtful feedback and Rachel Walther, who copyedited the manuscript. Finally, to my family—especially my wife, Ember, who offered steadfast encouragement and patience as well as her proofreading abilities—thank you.

FROM BLUE TO RED

1

INTRODUCTION

On the morning of Election Day in 2010, Democrats occupied three of the four Arkansas seats in the US House of Representatives, both US Senate seats, all state constitutional offices, and decisive majorities in both chambers of the Arkansas General Assembly. Within five years, Arkansas Republicans would hold all six US congressional positions, every state constitutional seat, and claim growing supermajorities in both state chambers. Over the next two election cycles, Republicans would enjoy unprecedented electoral success in Arkansas—the last remaining member of the once "Solid South" held by Democrats. By 2015, the Republican Party—the same party that failed to recruit candidates in many high-profile races as recently as 2010—not only held majorities in the state legislative chambers for the first time since Reconstruction but also had orchestrated one of the fastest, most powerful statewide political waves in the United States. In ten short years, from 2005 to 2015, the Natural State saw a dramatic, swift shift from Democratic Party majority control of government, stemming as far back as the nineteenth century, to Republican Party dominance.

Previously, Republicans had found success in regional pockets in the state, such as Northwest Arkansas, and occasionally took advantage of national political trends down ticket, but these wins were somewhat isolated and, in many cases, temporary.[1] For the most part, Arkansas remained stubbornly tied to the Democratic Party. While the dramatic shift in the partisan makeup of Arkansas officeholders may appear to have happened almost overnight, the rise of the Republicans in Arkansas was years, if not decades, in the making. From changes in voter preference at the top of the ticket in the 1960s to generational replacement in Arkansas's political power structure in the 1990s, and from party organizational strategies coming to fruition in the 2000s to a more nationalized and polarized electorate, *From Blue to Red* provides an in-depth analysis in its exploration of this noteworthy phenomenon—the rise of the Republican Party in Arkansas.

Since V. O. Key Jr.'s mid-twentieth-century study on southern politics, in which he wrote that, "perhaps in Arkansas we have the one-party system in its most undefiled and undiluted form," the state has been a fascination to political party scholars and those who study southern politics in particular.[2] While there were certainly surges of Republican political strength in the state since the mid-twentieth century, these were either isolated in presidential-election returns—a plurality of Arkansas voters has not favored a nonnative, non-southern Democratic candidate for president since John F. Kennedy in 1960—or brief aberrations at the state level. For example, Winthrop Rockefeller in 1966 and Frank White in 1980 each won gubernatorial races as Republicans but faced stiff Democratic opposition in the legislature and struggled to build the political base among Arkansas voters that a fledging organization's political longevity requires.

With exception to parts of Northwest Arkansas, which had pockets of Republican Party loyalists since the Civil War, the peculiar situation of Arkansas's politics had been that it remained largely a solid one-party Democratic state even as other southern states began the transition from Democratic Party domination to reliably Republican. While it is common for states, or even the federal government, to have periods of unified government—where the majority of the legislative branch and the leader of the executive branch are represented by the same party for a time—Arkansas's preference for Democratic candidates was historically consistent. The one-party dominance in the Natural State was not only noteworthy—it was, in fact, more enduring than any other in the United States.[3]

In the 1960s and 1970s, growing numbers of Arkansans began to prefer Republican presidential candidates at the top of the ballot, over any non-southern Democratic candidates. However, Arkansas continued to be one of the most Democratic states in the Union. This trend continued even as the twenty-first century approached. It was not as if Arkansas voters were uniquely liberal in their policy positions or views. Furthermore, the Democratic Party in the state was not, and had never been, particularly well organized, and Democratic officeholders were not ideologically consistent. To illustrate this point, in his review of Arkansas politics from 1960 to 1970, Jim Ranchino wrote, "Strange as it seems, Arkansas had no Democratic party organizations that functioned effectively at all levels of the state and local government after 1964. Arkansas existed politically as a no-party state."[4] Regardless, despite the lack of organization, and the growing number of Arkansans who sympathized with Republican candidates for president, the Democratic Party brand at the state level was the enduring, albeit weakening, link as Democratic elected officials remained careful to distinguish themselves and their views on issues from that of their partisan peers at the national level. Even Republican success at the state level, when achieved, was not independent of Democratic actions or missteps of the ruling party's making. Mike Huckabee, then only the state's third Republican governor since Reconstruction, ascended to the position in 1996 only after his predecessor—Jim Guy Tucker, a Democrat—resigned from office. Governor Huckabee, a popular state executive, was subsequently elected and reelected on his own and spent over ten years in office, while Democrats maintained many other constitutional offices and their century-old supermajorities in the General Assembly. All the while, other states in the southern United States were growing more and more Republican and switching longstanding majorities in their legislatures from Democratic to GOP control.[5] Meanwhile, with few exceptions, Arkansas remained Democratic.

In the 1990s and early 2000s, Arkansas, "the outlier," puzzled followers of politics and set the stage for countless conversations regarding the eventuality of becoming a "red state." Up until the 2010s, discussions among observers of Arkansas politics would often lead to two questions: Why had the state remained a Democratic stronghold even as such regional dominance by the party had long vanished in all other southern states? And, when, if ever, will Republicans finally enjoy the electoral success they had achieved in the rest of the South?

Though perhaps hard to imagine for someone who now only recognizes the contemporary state of Arkansas politics, these questions were relevant at the time as Arkansas continued to remain a state that strongly favored Democratic candidates at the federal and state levels of government. However, once the political landscape of Arkansas began to shift from Democratic to Republican Party dominance, the political balance of power in the Natural State changed in a big way, outpacing most other partisan shifts in modern US history. In the following chapters, I contextualize and analyze the recent and decisive rise of the Republican Party in Arkansas—one of the swiftest and most complete political shifts of US electoral politics in a state. An author of a project such as this stands upon the shoulders of others who have studied and helped distill Arkansas politics. Their excellent work helps make this task more manageable. Political scientists and historians have long studied Arkansas politics and have offered valuable insights into exploring the political behaviors and cultures that make up Natural State politics.[6] Beginning in the mid-twentieth century, the state's astute political observers began to describe the changing nature of voters in the Natural State. The long-standing ties to the Democratic Party for many southern states' predominantly white, conservative voters began to fray in the 1960s and 1970s as the national Democratic Party began to take stronger stances in favor of racial equality and socially liberal initiatives. At the same time, national Republicans saw an opportunity in southern states—for the first time in the twentieth century—to make significant headway by courting southern conservatives to their party. This period also began to see partisan sorting (whereby more Americans rightward of the median voter began to consistently identify with the Republican Party and those leftward of the median associated with the Democratic Party) taking place in all parts of the United States, but it was slow to take root in southern states and even slower in Arkansas.[7]

This more leftward push on some issues by the national Democratic Party, coupled with aggressive attempts by Republicans to court southern conservatives in general, resulted in efforts by Democratic candidates in the Natural State to distinguish their own, and the state's, Democratic brand from that of the national party. At this time, Ranchino's assessment of Arkansas voters in the 1960s suggested steady one-party domination persisted, in part, because Arkansans favored the perceived "better man" among candidates who disproportionally competed in Democratic Party primaries. Diane Blair emphasized the demographics, economics, and political history of Arkansas as reasons for the continued political tradition of Democratic Party support—particularly at the state level.[8] A peripheral southern state with a relatively low proportion of African American voters and a politics notably less vocally centralized around notions of white supremacy than neighboring Mississippi and some other states in the region, Arkansas was somewhat insulated from the race-baiting politics that largely defined Democratic politics in other former Confederate states. This approach, in part, allowed office seekers to avoid taking polarizing stances on issues such as race and continue to operate in a moderate political space while avoiding positions on particularly sensitive national issues. In addition, Blair noted the emergence of "the Big Three" in Arkansas politics—Dale Bumpers, David Pryor, and Bill Clinton—in the last quarter of the twentieth century and contended that their leadership styles, effective campaigning, and charisma managed to prolong Democratic Party success in Arkansas despite significant Republican gains in other southern states in the 1980s and 1990s.[9]

Moving into the 1990s and early twenty-first century, scholarly work examined the continuation of Arkansans favoring Republicans for president, and in some cases, governor: more frequently adopting the self-identified label of "independent" over "Democrat," and all the while still often supporting—particularly in state and local races—the Democratic Party.[10] Meanwhile, signs of Republican Party electoral success were beginning to emerge in Arkansas, albeit more slowly than most everywhere else in the South. Following the 1992 elections—when Arkansas governor Bill Clinton was elected president of the United States—Arkansas voters elected two Republicans to their four US House of Representatives seats. In 1996, one of those House members, Tim Hutchinson, was elected to the US Senate, the first Republican in Arkansas to hold that position since Reconstruction. However, these gains paled in comparison to those made by the GOP in neighboring states. Observing the mid-1990s GOP gains in Arkansas and elsewhere in the South, Earl and Merle Black wrote, "Arkansas had the weakest Republican party in the Peripheral South."[11] Of course we now know, in roughly two decades the state's preference for Republican elected officials would usher in a tidal wave of GOP electoral gains.

Despite the excellent scholarship previously focused on the state, until now no single source has yet offered an in-depth, scholarly examination of one of the most significant political developments in the history of Arkansas politics—the sudden and overwhelming rise of the Republican Party in Arkansas.

Apart from the rapidity in which this dramatic partisan shift occurred from the early 2000s to 2015, there are at least two other reasons why the recent emergence of the Republican Party in Arkansas is worth studying. First, parties are essential for democracy. While political parties and partisanship are often bemoaned by voters and observers alike, E. E. Schattschneider once wrote, "The political parties created democracy and modern democracy is unthinkable save in terms of the parties."[12] It is most often through parties that we facilitate the emergence of differences of policy positions, organize government, inform voters in the form of cues by partisan positions, and recruit candidates. Second, the essential nature of parties for democracy assumes there is more than one party competing for votes and power. A period of time in which one party dominates as completely as the Democratic Party in Arkansas did for well over a century does not result in a strong single party, but instead practically no party in the traditional sense of the word. It is a simple equation: democracy requires parties and parties require interparty competition.

On one hand, the Democratic Party of Arkansas was not organized in the traditional sense of the word, and was largely based on factions built around personalities rather than ideas. On the other, the Republican Party—for much of its history in the state—was a party in name only that regularly failed to recruit candidates for office. Historically, the relative nonexistence of the GOP in Arkansas resulted in heated, crowded Democratic primaries, determining the inevitable conclusion of a general election months prior to November of an election year. However, over the last four decades, Republicans in Arkansas began to: strengthen their formal organizational structure, recruit stronger candidates, coordinate and fundraise more effectively, create messages that resonated with a growing proportion of the Arkansas electorate, leverage national partisan trends that would benefit them or disadvantage Democratic candidates in the state, and seize on strategic errors made by the other party. The story of the rise of the Republican Party in Arkansas—whether the result of collective political genius, accident, inevitable external pressures, or a mix of all three—essentially results in a state political environment where, for the first time in well over a century, and only for a brief moment, Arkansas had two viable, competitive parties, before the once overwhelmingly Democratic state became solidly Republican.

The purpose of this book is to chronicle one of the most dramatic state-level partisan shifts in modern US history; to document and attempt to explain how and why this shift occurred, to measure its impact on the state's politics, and explore what it means for the future of Arkansas politics and policy. To account for this rapid ascendance into state political leadership, while also recognizing the previous decades that provide the context and framework for more recent success, the Republican Party of Arkansas will be assessed through the lens of three "generations" categorized by time periods from the 1960s to today.

While the following chapters present data and findings in varied forms, I believe the most significant sources of information on the topic of the rise of the GOP in Arkansas are the firsthand accounts obtained through interviews. Thanks to the David and Barbara Pryor Center for Oral and Visual History project, this book offers unique insights from those who witnessed the dramatic partisan shift in Arkansas: reporters, academics, party officials, and elected office holders. The individuals interviewed by me on behalf of the Pryor Center provided invaluable information and unique perspectives on the partisan change in the state. Many of these individuals are quoted in the following chapters, but all contributed to the framing of this study. (A note that these Pryor Center interviews have been edited for length and clarity.)

The organization of this book is inspired by the highly influential scholar of southern politics and political behavior V. O. Key Jr., who wrote on the tripartite nature of political party as party-in-the-electorate, party organization, and party-in-government.[13] Key's organization of the concept of "party" encompasses the multiple elements of a political party's structure, function, and purposes. This book borrows from this organizational conceptualization of a political party. In order to introduce the reader to these three facets of a political party in a way that recognizes the evolution of the state's partisan politics over several decades, I have organized the time between the 1966 gubernatorial election of Winthrop Rockefeller to the present day into three distinct periods or generations. Throughout the book, the three parts of a political party are framed within these three generations of the modern Arkansas Republican Party.

Chapter two provides the timeline and organizational structure by which the modern Arkansas Republican Party has evolved from the mid-1960s to today. From the election of Winthrop Rockefeller in 1966, the first Republican governor since Reconstruction, to 2022, the Republican Party has gone from a fledgling organization in a state dominated by the one-party political climate of the "Solid South" to, it is argued, one of the most Republican states in the Union today.[14] In a 2019 interview, Arkansas Republican Party chairman Doyle Webb said, "I will assert that we are now the most Republican state of the 50 states. . . . How so? Because our federal delegation is fully Republican. If you look at the other red states, you don't always see that. Many of our sister states realize that we got here the quickest as well." He goes on, "There's 168 members of the RNC; three from every state and then three from each of the six territories. There was a time when it was, 'Where is Arkansas? Oh, it's by Texas.' Well, now people know where Arkansas is. I believe that we could be the reddest of all the states."[15] Chapter two provides an overview and structure for conceptualizing this dramatic shift over three periods in time.

The third chapter reviews the political behavior of the Arkansas electorate from the first generation of the modern GOP in Arkansas to the present day. The state goes from an electorate that overwhelmingly, top to bottom, elected Democrats to practically every office, to a public known

Table 1.1
Interviewees for From Blue to Red: The Rise of the GOP in Arkansas

Jeff Weaver	Former congressional staff / former campaign manager
Roby Brock	Former gubernatorial staff / journalist
Rex Nelson	Former gubernatorial staff / journalist
Tim Griffin	Former US congressman / former lieutenant governor / attorney general
Ann Clemmer	Party activist / former state legislator
Skip Rutherford	Former congressional staff / former Democratic Party chair
Doyle Webb	Former state legislator / former Republican Party chair
Shane Broadway	Former state legislator / former candidate for lieutenant governor
John Brummett	Journalist
Jay Barth	Professor of political science
Bill Vickery	Political advisor
Asa Hutchinson	Former congressman / former Republican Party chair / former governor
Hal Bass	Professor of political science
Mike Huckabee	Former lieutenant governor / former governor
Mike Beebe	Former state legislator / former attorney general / former governor
Davy Carter	Former state legislator
Janine A. Parry	Professor of political science
Angie Maxwell	Professor of political science
Wesley Clark	Retired US Army general / former Democratic candidate for president
Laura Kellams	Former journalist

for its independent streak and ticket-splitting practices of supporting GOP presidential nominees and favoring Democrats lower on the ballot, to finally a statewide electorate that, with few exceptions, largely advantages Republicans in virtually every level of government. The roots underpinning Democratic dominance were slowly eroding as early as the 1960s but were not fully realized until much later as the national brand of the Democratic Party brand weakened among Arkansans. Using election results, public opinion polling, and interviews from Arkansans who witnessed this shift firsthand, chapter three produces a glimpse into the collective electoral behavior of the Arkansas voters, the strategic maneuvers that strengthened the GOP state party organization—enabling it to capitalize on a changing political climate and shape a more consistent party brand—and the policy impact of Republican officials over time that, more recently, governs at virtually every level of Arkansas government.

Chapter four explores the roles and functions of the two major state party organizations in Arkansas. Statewide party organizations are an often overlooked part of a state's partisan political landscape. For most of the twentieth century, Arkansas politics saw a loose, decentralized, informal Democratic structure built around personal loyalties—the result of one-party dominance for decades. Republicans, on the other hand, struggled mightily to gain a critical mass of co-partisans to be able to claim a statewide organization in any real sense. That is, until Winthrop Rockefeller used his own personal wealth to fund such an effort in the 1960s. However, the sudden and sustained partisan shift in Arkansas seen over the last decade suggests party organizations played a role in developing the partisan dynamics of the state today. The survey-based analysis in chapter four permits two snapshots in time—the first, in the second generation of the GOP in Arkansas and the second, in the current era—in order to analyze the extent to which the party organizations played a role in the rise of the modern GOP in Arkansas. While Arkansas Democrats enjoyed incredibly stable electoral success, perhaps due to the nature of its political dominance, the party lacked organization as election outcomes were more or less settled upon personality rather than policy or recruitment of talent among formal party officials. However, beginning in the last decade of the twentieth century, the Arkansas Republican Party began to build an electoral juggernaut that soon surpassed the organization apparatus of Democrats in the state—planting the seeds for future electoral success. This chapter compares survey data from a 1999 study to a 2013 examination of state party organizations to evaluate the changes that have taken place with regard to the operations and organizational strength of both state parties in a time of political change in the Natural State.[16]

While the partisan shift in political power in Arkansas is apparent, the policy implications of such a shift are less obvious. What, if any, were the immediate shifts in legislative behavior and policy outputs following the Republican takeover of the Arkansas General Assembly for the first time since Reconstruction? How did this political upheaval impact the interplay between the state's executive and legislative branches? How does the introduction of a state politics more focused on national issues impact policymaking for the party in power? Chapter five explores the breadth and impact of the partisan shift on governing and policymaking at the state level by comparing data on legislative sessions immediately before and after Republicans claimed majorities in the General Assembly and sharing firsthand accounts from elected officials.

Political party scholars have long contended that competitive parties are important components of a democratic government. Given the state's historical one-party dominance by Democrats, and the considerable strength currently exhibited among Republicans in the state's politics, has Arkansas simply traded one party's dominance for another? Chapter six concludes the book and visits this question while considering the complicating factor of the state's current political landscape in the face of inevitable demographic changes.

The following chapters examine the events leading up to and the resultant actions of the rise of the Republican Party in Arkansas by looking at both major parties through the lens of its electorate, each party's organizational structures and reforms, and the elements of change and stability within the state government of Arkansas over the last several decades. While the purpose of this study is on Arkansas politics specifically, I am hopeful the following chapters will offer a framework for broader application. Partisan change at the state level is not exclusive to one state.

2

THE THREE GENERATIONS OF THE GOP IN ARKANSAS

The First Generation: 1966 to 1992

It is important to recognize that while the sudden and overwhelming shift to a dominant Republican Party in Arkansas occurred within an astonishingly short amount of time, the emergence of the party—from practical nonexistence to respectable minority party to majority status— occurred over decades. I posit that the modern Republican Party in the state has seen three distinct generations.

I propose that the first generation of the modern Republican Party in Arkansas began in 1966 with the statewide election of Winthrop Rockefeller, the first Republican governor in Arkansas since Reconstruction, and of then-chairman of the Arkansas Republican Party, John Paul Hammerschmidt, to the US House of Representatives. Governor Rockefeller, who first ran and lost in 1964, would be reelected to another two-year term in 1968, only to lose a bid for a third term in 1970. Not long after leaving the governor's mansion, Rockefeller was diagnosed with cancer and died in 1973. At the time of his death, the party he had spent well over a decade building had largely returned to its former, noncompetitive self. While the 1966 elections of Rockefeller and Hammerschmidt marked a historical milestone for Arkansas and the state Republican Party, it was Representative Hammerschmidt who alone became the perennially dominant Republican in Arkansas— serving his Northwest Arkansas district until his retirement in 1993.

By the mid-twentieth century, Arkansas was regarded as one of the most one-party-dominated states in the United States.[1] As in most other former Confederate states, post-Reconstruction control of the levers of state political power were almost solely in the hands of Democrats in Arkansas. Republicans in the state, outside of a few hamlets in Northwest Arkansas and the River Valley, were few and far between. The scant numbers of Republicans in the state were called "Post Office Republicans" due to the perception that the fledgling organization was comprised of small numbers of partisans whose primary interest was to dole out patronage on behalf of Republican presidential administrations.[2] At this time in the state's political history, Arkansas had not had a Republican governor or US senator since Reconstruction.

The new would-be party standard-bearer was Winthrop Rockefeller. Rockefeller settled in Arkansas in the 1950s and quickly became active in local and state politics and policy. An heir to one of the richest families in the Unites States at the time, Rockefeller had no familial connections to Arkansas, but on the advice of a friend and fellow World War II veteran he sought refuge in the state to escape a life of excess and scandal in New York. Discussing Rockefeller's move to Arkansas and his subsequent impact on the state's politics, Rex Nelson said, "Arkansas saved Winthrop Rockefeller and Winthrop Rockefeller saved Arkansas."[3] In 1955, Governor Orval Faubus, early in his first term in office, appointed Rockefeller chairman of the Arkansas Industrial Development Commission—at the time, a newly formed body intended to help draw business and industry investment into the state.

Throughout his time on the commission, Rockefeller involved himself in efforts to rebuild the Republican Party in Arkansas and promote the importance of a competitive two-party system in the state. He also invested considerable sums of money from his personal wealth to support Republican candidates in Arkansas in the 1960 and 1962 election cycles.[4] By 1962, Rockefeller's investment in the beleaguered party appeared to be inspiring more Arkansans to run as Republicans. In that election cycle, more people filed to run for office in the state as Republicans than in any other election year since Reconstruction, and Rockefeller personally funded the campaigns of twenty-two Republicans seeking state legislative positions.[5] According to John Ward, author of *The Arkansas Rockefeller*, during this time Rockefeller was actively advocating for a two-party system in Arkansas and was quoted by the *Arkansas Democrat* as saying on radio and television programs the following:

> When I advocate an active, virile two-party system I do so in the firm conviction that Arkansas as a state and Arkansans as individuals will benefit from it. Your freedom will be expanded. Your horizons will be broadened. And we will achieve a new significance in the Nation. We will cease being taken for granted. I urge you to join in the work that lies ahead—not just two or four years ahead, but in the immediate future, to construct a meaningful, exciting second party for this great state. There are marvelous times ahead for free Americans, free Arkansans. Be part of them.[6]

Rockefeller, the most prominent Republican in the state at the time, would continue to serve in the Faubus administration until his resignation on March 28, 1964—the year he launched his first campaign for governor.[7]

Two years before Rockefeller would become the first Republican governor of Arkansas in the twentieth century, he would run for the same office and lose. However, his losing bid would establish him, a Republican, as a viable candidate going into 1966. If Rockefeller began the 1964 campaign for governor as an underdog to five-term Democratic incumbent Faubus—which he surely did—intraparty conflicts also troubled the state Republican standard-bearer. The 1964 campaign for governor highlighted the divisions within his party—largely along lines between the old guard members of the perennial party out of government and those associated with Rockefeller's efforts. These issues were further complicated by the fact that Winthrop's brother, Nelson, was seeking the Republican presidential nomination in the same year—placing the Rockefellers at odds with Barry Goldwater, who became the eventual GOP nominee in 1964 to run against President Lyndon Johnson. The national party's politics spilled into the state party's once Winthrop endorsed his brother—several months before Nelson would officially announce his bid to run.[8] With Goldwater, an opponent of the Civil Rights Act of 1964, becoming the eventual nominee for president, the issue of race became a key factor in the gubernatorial contest. Faubus also opposed to the Civil Rights Act, but it appeared Rockefeller's views differed from Goldwater's. Rockefeller presented himself as a racial moderate, who opposed the national government's policing powers granted by the Civil Rights Act but walked a delicate line that distanced himself from his party's wing of Goldwater supporters—endearing him to racial moderates, progressive voters in the state, and African Americans.[9] However, the results of the 1964 contest mirrored the state's final tabulations for the presidential race, with a victory for the Democratic candidate, albeit by a narrower margin than expected in a solidly Democratic state. Although Rockefeller lost in 1964, his 43 percent share of the vote was the highest for a Republican in the twentieth century to date.

Rockefeller faced his 1964 loss by immediately announcing his bid to run in 1966. This time, he was the clear leader of his party, and the Democrats, seeking to fill a power vacuum with the absence of six-term governor Orval Faubus, saw a seven-man contest for the party nomination. A crowded Democratic field to replace Faubus could have led to an energetic and even raucous campaign cycle, but, according to Jim Ranchino, this was not the case. He wrote, "A searing heat wave struck the state a month before the election, but it didn't help to heat up the political climate. That summer's activities provided the voters with one of the dullest campaigns in recent history."[10] Democratic primary voters settled on an outspoken segregationist, Jim Johnson, whose appeal was largely among white voters who agreed with him on the issue of race—alienating racial moderates and Blacks. Rockefeller received 90 percent of votes cast by Black voters.

Perhaps in all but one respect, Rockefeller communicated the same campaign message in 1966 that he did in 1964, advocating for the reform of state government in the post-Faubus era. While Rockefeller may have struggled to articulate a clear position on the matter of civil rights in 1964, in 1966 his views on the issue were a stark contrast to the racist rhetoric of the Democrat nominee Johnson. In hindsight, the dramatic and historic shift in Arkansas voting behavior—electing a Republican for governor—was all but a foregone conclusion the moment Democrats gave Johnson the party nomination. According to Ranchino, following Johnson's nomination the GOP faithful knew they had a chance in 1966: "There was much rejoicing among Republicans the night Jim Johnson became the Democratic nominee for Governor."[11] In the end, moderate and liberal Democrats, African Americans, and Republicans carried Rockefeller to victory with 54.4 percent of the overall vote.

Rockefeller's victory, while an electoral triumph of historic proportion, was somewhat hallowed by the lack of success for the GOP in countless other races in the state. With exception to John Paul Hammerschmidt's first election win in the Third Congressional District (the beginning of a decades-long career representing the Northwest Arkansas district in Washington, DC), and Maurice "Footsie" Britt's election to the office of lieutenant governor, very little of the partisan makeup of the state was altered in 1966. In his first session of the General Assembly, Rockefeller was met with a hostile, overwhelmingly Democratic legislature. In her study on Rockefeller's time as governor, Cathy Kunzinger Urwin describes the frustrations experienced by Rockefeller at the hands of Democrats in the legislature, as well as by some traditional Republicans outside the realm of governmental power.[12] Despite these challenges, and perhaps again due to the Democrats' disregarding voter's apprehensions in nominating another candidate unpalatable to the state's electorate, Rockefeller was granted a second two-year term in 1968.

However, opposition and controversy filled his second term in office. The Democratic General Assembly was determined to not permit him political victories in the way of reforms, and the electoral opposition of an impressive Democratic upstart named Dale Bumpers—who, like Rockefeller, was a progressive breath of fresh air in a state still dominated by the shadow of Faubus—resulted in Rockefeller losing his second reelection bid to Bumpers in 1970. The GOP losses did not stop there. The cycle seemed to knock the air out of their sails and steal any hope of the party gaining momentum into the new decade. Also, the cycle served as a reminder that the state Republican Party's successes in the second half of the 1960s—despite their historic nature—were largely limited to Rockefeller and did not extend beyond him in a way that led to substantial development of the party in the state. In his account of the 1970 election, Richard Yates described the results for GOP candidates running for state and local positions in Arkansas as a "debacle" and pointed out that, of all the GOP candidates seeking statewide office, including forty-six who ran for seats in either the House or the Senate, only two were elected to the General Assembly.[13]

In addition to being the first Republican governor of Arkansas since Reconstruction, Rockefeller's financial support of the state party and his attempts to usher in a more progressive element challenged the party's status quo. However, despite the newly invigorated efforts at party organization and Rockefeller's own electoral victories, intraparty conflicts regarding the direction of the party and Rockefeller's own struggles working with a solid Democratic majority in the General Assembly left the Arkansas Republicans firmly entrenched as a weak, albeit strengthening, minority party.[14]

While Rockefeller's own electoral success resulted in his party claiming the governor's office for four years (1967–71), much of his appeal to voters was not shared by his party members. His base of political support was largely among progressive Democrats, the few Republicans in the state, and African Americans who had grown weary of Faubus and other southern Democrats' stances on race issues.[15] Opinions about

Rockefeller's role in the evolution of the state's politics are mixed. It cannot be denied that he was the architect of the Republican Party—as it has been known for the last several decades—and he undoubtedly deserves credit for bringing life to an all but dormant Republican Party organization in Arkansas. Other than his own electoral successes, perhaps Rockefeller's most significant contribution to the GOP and—as a result, his quest for a two-party state—was the increase in Republicans competing for elected office in Arkansas over the 1960s. For example, the 1966, 1968, and 1970 election cycles saw thirty-six, thirty, and thirty-nine House seats contested in the general elections, respectively—three cycles of general election competition not seen for years, nor again until decades later. Likewise, contested elections in the general election for the Senate were also higher during this period.[16] However, his personal political victories failed to translate to lasting success, via electoral victories in these contested races that led to sustained political momentum. Reflecting on Rockefeller's political impact, historian Tom Dillard wrote, "Without a doubt his greatest defeat was the failure to develop a viable two-party system. The governor succeeded in building a large personal following, but he was unable to transfer that support to his party."[17] Despite his efforts as a party organizer, candidate, and elected official, his personal political success did not transform the partisan dynamics of the state in a way that created lasting change.

Following Rockefeller's absence from the governor's mansion in 1971 and death in 1973, the Republican Party found itself in much the same condition as ten years before. A comparison of the party's success between Rockefeller's first election bid and the first part of the new decade show that the GOP had made only nominal gains in the state legislature—with a handful of Republican House of Representatives and even fewer in the state's Senate chamber—with no Republicans holding a statewide constitutional office. Despite dramatic growth in the number of candidates filing to run as Republicans for elected office in Arkansas in the 1960s, few managed to claim electoral victory. Hammerschmidt, the only long-standing electoral success for Republicans in this era, continued to be reelected to the US House of Representatives. In fact, it could be argued that Hammerschmidt was the one remaining bright spot for the GOP in the state from the 1960s that remained in the 1970s (and beyond). In 1974, Congressman Hammerschmidt beat a young upstart named Bill Clinton, becoming one of only two people to defeat the eventual president of the United States in an election.

There appear to be clear reasons why Rockefeller's success failed to translate into many GOP victories in Arkansas in the 1970s. First, and most obvious to students of southern politics, his electoral base of support was not solely made up of a majority of loyal Republicans, but of Democrats and self-identified independents. Based on surveys he conducted in 1968 and 1970 among Arkansas voters, Ranchino reported that nearly 60 percent of those polled reported either identifying as "strong Democrat" or "not very strong Democrat" and 24 percent claimed to be "independent"—leaving a meager 17 percent reporting to be "strong Republican" or "not very strong Republican."[18] While these figures were compiled over two electoral cycles spanning as many years, and there are obvious issues with deriving too much from survey data of this brief a period, it illustrates the partisan political demographics in play at the time. Additionally, in the late 1960s and early 1970s, Arkansas voters first began to engage with "the Big Three"—Dale Bumpers, David Pryor, and Bill Clinton—young, charismatic, progressive Democrats who revitalized their party and allowed it to move beyond the Faubus years of the 1950s and 1960s. It stands to reason that a great many among the Rockefeller base of voters shifted to the likes of the Big Three and their acolytes over the years—effectively stifling any lasting GOP gains at the state and local levels.

The 1970s marked a point in time when the voting behavior of the Arkansas electorate was changing. Perhaps as a reaction to the Democratic Party's national thrust toward civil rights, the social liberalization of the party's national agenda, or both, Arkansans began moving toward Republican presidential candidates while continuing to largely favor Democrats lower on the ticket during the early part of the decade—a trend that would continue with exception only to a southern Democratic candidate for the nation's highest office. This shift of consistently favoring Republican presidential candidates over non-southern Democratic nominees began in 1972, but Arkansas voters' disapproval of national Democratic politics was apparent in 1968 with the plurality of voters supporting segregationist governor of Alabama and former Democrat George Wallace as he ran for president atop the American Independent Party ticket.

The practice of voting for the Republican presidential nominee while still largely favoring Democratic candidates down the ticket, or ticket-splitting, provided a window of opportunity for state Republicans, as Democrats in Arkansas were faced with the challenge of distancing themselves from their national party's stances—a practice the Big Three developed into something of a political art form in the 1970s, 1980s, and 1990s. In her study of these three iconic Democrats who are credited, in part, with stemming the tide of Republican gains in the state until their political ambitions or political retirements pulled them from state politics, Blair wrote that these men, of whom at least one appeared on the ballot every cycle between 1970 and 1994, helped maintain Democratic political power in the state while its neighbors began the process of historic partisan change in the 1980s and 1990s.[19] Blair further elaborated on this idea when she wrote, "What is being suggested here is that the cumulative draw of the Big Three at the top of the ticket sustained and strengthened the popularity of the Democratic label in Arkansas, thereby withstanding the general southern trend toward Republican realignment."[20] Thus, ticket-splitting, which advantaged Republican presidential candidates in Arkansas beginning in the 1970s, did not translate to meaningful gains for Republicans in other state and local races during this time.

Blair wrote of the shift, "Aided by widespread ticket-splitting, Republicans have moved from a position of utter hopelessness through the 1940s to a somewhat more respectable, but still sub competitive position in the 1950s to an occasional gubernatorial victory and seeming presidential advantage by the 1980s."[21] Regarding ticket-splitting in Arkansas, Blair pointed out that the 1972 election cycle in particular, when all seventy-five of the state's counties went for Republican Richard Nixon's reelection for president and Democrat Dale Bumper's reelection for governor.

The latter part of the decade saw a historic election victory for the GOP and, for a time, resulted in two of the four Arkansas seats in the US House of Representatives becoming occupied by Republicans. The Second Congressional District seat, occupied by Jim Guy Tucker, was open in 1978, due to the one-term House member seeking the Democratic nomination for senator. That open seat resulted in four Democrats competing for the nomination—the winner of which faced Republican candidate Ed Bethune. Bethune, a Korean War veteran, former FBI agent, and former prosecutor, had lost his 1972 bid for the office of attorney general to Tucker, but in 1978 he would be victorious when he sought the office being vacated by his former foe. Bethune beat Democratic nominee Doug Brandon 48.8 percent to 51.2 percent.[22] Much like Hammerschmidt's victory in Northwest Arkansas the decade prior, Bethune's win of the US House seat representing Central Arkansas was a historic moment for the state and the GOP; Bethune was the first Republican to represent the Second District in over a century. Bethune would go on to successfully defend the Second District congressional seat in 1980 and 1982.

In the early 1970s, the state's voters had shifted their presidential preferences toward Republicans. Meanwhile, the rank and file among the Arkansas GOP struggled to manage growing divides among waning numbers of Rockefeller Republicans and the growing contingent of the party seeking more conservative voices such as Ronald Reagan, who first sought his party's nomination for president in 1976 and lost to incumbent Gerald Ford. According to Blair, at the close of the decade, primarily through party procedural processes, the activists within the Republican Party of Arkansas had thwarted the remaining progressives within the party and began supporting the national party's growing conservative posture.[23] In describing this time, she wrote, "As long as Rockefeller led the Arkansas Republicans, the party had a progressive, reformist cast, and those whom Rockefeller had brought into the party continued to dominate party offices and shape presidential preferences until 1980. After Reagan's sweeping nomination victory and subsequent election, however, power within the Arkansas GOP switched sharply to the right."[24]

At this time, the Arkansas General Assembly, comprised of one hundred seats in the state's House of Representatives and thirty-five seats in the Senate, had proven to be nearly impenetrable for the GOP. However, the midterm election of 1978 produced an impressive number of Republicans contesting seats (forty-one House seats and two of eighteen Senate seats), with a historically unprecedented number of Republicans competing at the state legislative level.[25] While these contested seats resulted in few gains in the legislature, the level of interest to run as a Republican for state representative seats must have led the GOP to be optimistic as the state approached the 1980s.

In 1980, Arkansas voters narrowly chose Reagan for president. Arkansans had already begun to favor Republicans for president in 1972 and had embarked on what would become a decades-long practice of often opting for the GOP at the top of the ticket. Reflecting on the state's shift to Republican presidential candidates, Blair and Robert Savage wrote, "If the last twenty elections are divided into twenty-year cycles, the decline of Democratic presidential fortunes is a dramatic one."[26] However, the real historic moment was the GOP victory over incumbent governor Bill Clinton. Clinton suffered the loss after one term in office at the hands of Frank White, a banker, former Air Force pilot, and former head of the Arkansas Industrial Development Commission (now, the Arkansas Economic Development Commission) under Democratic governor David Pryor.

White's surprise victory over the charismatic Rhodes scholar was more a rebuke of Clinton than approval of White or the Republican platform. Clinton's term had been marred by a riot among Cuban refugees, who had been assigned to a military base in the state by President Carter, garnering widespread negative media attention and criticism from a weary Arkansas public who aimed their frustrations and fears at the governor. White was not well-known when he filed to run against Clinton, but he was an established businessman and conducted an aggressive campaign—one that would put him in the governor's office, only the second time a Republican had held the position since Reconstruction. With half of the US House delegation, a Republican in the governor's mansion, and Arkansans favoring the Republican president in the White House, there were reasons to believe the GOP was finally making lasting gains in the state. However, despite his historic and surprising victory, Governor White served only one term—losing the 1982 midterm election to Bill Clinton. Following the 1982 election, Clinton would go on to seek, and win, the same office in 1984, 1986, and 1990.[27]

The 1980s saw only modest to marginal gains for Republicans in the General Assembly. Despite the increase in competitive legislative seats in 1978, Republicans only contested an average of fifteen of the one hundred House seats in the 1980s and only two out of the seventeen or eighteen seats up for election in the Senate every two years in the 1980, 1984, 1986, and 1988 cycles.[28] Compared to the Rockefeller years of the second half of the 1960s, at least in measuring the number of contested races in the state House and Senate, the GOP appeared to be backsliding.

Congressman Bethune did not seek reelection for his US House seat (which would be won by a Democrat) in 1984, and instead ran against Democratic incumbent Pryor for the US Senate—a race he would lose by a margin of nearly 15 percent.[29] Following his defeat at the polls, Bethune was elected as the state GOP chairman where, over the two years in which he served his state's party organization, he "revamped the party in the state" by focusing the party's attention on recruitment for competition in local races.[30]

Recalling the apparent opportunity for political momentum, in favor of the perennial party out of power at the close of the 1970s and dawn of the 1980s, Gary Wekkin wrote "The 1980s began full of hope and promise for Arkansas Republicans. . . . But it was not meant to be."[31] The decade ended with relatively few/minor sustained, measurable gains for the GOP in Arkansas. Despite another decade of split-ticket voting by way of supporting GOP presidential candidates in all three general elections in the 1980s, Arkansans still favored Democratic incumbents at the state and local levels. However, a gubernatorial victory and Bethune's electoral successes in the Second Congressional District showed that, for a time, Arkansas voters could entertain the idea of choosing Republicans if the conditions where right or, in the case of Clinton in 1980, if they sought to punish the Democratic incumbent. Despite the decade not shaping up the way Republicans in the state might have hoped, the 1980s certainly highlighted a change among the Arkansas electorate—they were not switching their voting habits from Democratic to Republican, but had begun to act more and more like independent voters.[32] In their review of public opinion surveys from 1962 to 1986, Blair and Savage noted a decline of Arkansans identifying as Democrats and an increasing number who identified as independents. Based on their calculations of survey data compiled over the decade, approximately half of Arkansans identified as Democrats, roughly one in five Arkansans considered themselves Republicans, and over a quarter claimed to be independent. This trend would maintain in the coming decade and accelerate in the next century.

Still within the first generation of the modern Republican Party, 1990 found the state GOP lagging behind its southern neighbors as many other former Confederate states' voters had begun what political scientists call a secular realignment—a gradual shift from one party identification and loyalty to another. However, the year marked notable changes within the state's politics and set the course for a series of historic occurrences over the course of the following decade.

In 1990, Governor Clinton, who had served from 1979–81 and again since 1983, had concluded his first four-year term in office since voters had approved a constitutional amendment extending gubernatorial term limits in 1984. Over the second half of the 1980s, Clinton had increased his presence in national Democratic circles by positioning himself as a centrist problem-solver who worked outside of his national party's more liberal ideals. By 1988, as outgoing chair of the National Governors Association, he was considered a potential candidate for president and spoke at a prominent time during the Democratic National Convention that year. Though he did not choose to run for president in 1988, there was considerable speculation that he would, in fact, seek his party's nomination in 1992. This speculation complicated his reelection bid in 1990. If reelected, would he carry out the full, four-year term? Would he be focused on Arkansans or his own progressive political ambitions? Meanwhile, Republican voters faced, arguably for the first time, two politically prominent and electorally viable gubernatorial candidates competing for the Republican nomination that year: Tommy Robinson and Sheffield Nelson.

Later that fall, Clinton would go on to win his final reelection bid for governor and, despite pledges on the campaign trail that he would not run for president in 1992, almost immediately began to put together a team to consider the viability of a presidential run.[33] The gubernatorial contest in 1990 is historically significant to the Arkansas Republican Party for two reasons. First, it secured Governor Clinton's reelection bid and set in motion his presidential victory in 1992. This, as I argue later, provided an opportunity for the GOP to gain momentum in the state, eventually leading to over ten consecutive years of Republican state executive leadership. Second, the 1990 GOP primary contest of Robinson and Nelson brought significant attention to the state's Republican politics for the first time; and, through their competing styles and backgrounds, the two candidates—both former Democrats—helped rebrand both parties in a way that would eventually benefit the GOP.

The first generation of the modern Republican Party in Arkansas stretches over more than thirty years, beginning with Rockefeller's historic gubernatorial victories in 1966 and again in 1968, with his robust personal investments supporting a party that, despite these efforts, failed to achieve sustained growth in terms of recruitment or overall political success. The 1970s and 1980s consist of election cycles with relatively low numbers of Republicans seeking offices and, with rare exception, virtually none winning. However, looking back over this period, and considering where the party began—as something almost less than a minority party, more like a third party in a one-party state—the first generation yielded positive, albeit modest, gains for the GOP in Arkansas.

By the end of this first generation, Republicans could claim two governors, a handful of US Representatives (one well established in a district even deemed electorally "safe" by every practical measure), a (very) slow increase in state legislators, and, most importantly, weaker Democratic party loyalty among the Arkansas electorate, resulting in ticket-splitting to the benefit of Republican presidential candidates. Despite, once again, being on the losing side of a gubernatorial contest in 1990, the Republican Party of Arkansas had already begun to construct a powerful narrative that the Democratic Party was out of sync with Arkansas voters—a point of fact, if only reflected by the state's shift to favoring Republican presidential candidates—and that Republicans could, like many Democrats in the state before, tap into the populist impulses of many Arkansas voters. Over the next two decades, the nationalizing of the Democratic Party in the eyes of the Arkansas electorate (despite the best efforts of Democrats in the state to avoid it) cultivated a political base among populist conservatives in Arkansas, who capitalized on Democratic missteps; this was a move that would eventually bear fruit for the GOP in the state.

While the country's political environment struggled to adapt to the social changes of the 1960s and 1970s, and the Democratic Party's national identity became more openly liberal on stances such as civil rights, gender equality, and spending on social programs, there were early signs of Arkansas voters' disapproval of this new national brand. Rockefeller's victory in 1966, due in large part to the support of a mix of progressive Republicans, reform-minded Democrats, and African Americans, all opposed to the old guard of the state's Democratic Party, signaled an independent streak in the state's voters. In 1968, as Rockefeller won reelection as governor, Arkansans produced perhaps the strangest mix of preferences in state electoral history—favoring the progressive Republican Rockefeller, the reelection of Vietnam War critic J. William Fulbright to the Senate, and granting electoral college votes to the independent candidacy of Alabama segregationist George Wallace for president. Moving into the early 1970s, as Democrats in other states began to witness the beginning of a slow decline in political dominance in the Solid South, one might have assumed Arkansas would not be far behind the trend of its neighboring states in the former Confederacy. However, the end of the first generation of the modern Arkansas Republican Party marks the beginning of an era marked by three young, reform-minded Democrats: Dale Bumpers, David Pryor, and Bill Clinton, or, as Diane Blair referred to them, "the Big Three." Each of them possessed a unique style that would serve them remarkably well in the coming decades as they balanced their political identities as Democrats in a state where the majority of voters were becoming less tied to the party's national brand.

While the party had witnessed electoral successes not yet seen before in the twentieth century, this first generation fell short of building on these successes in a way that created a consistent electoral momentum. Rather, this period is filled with a series of triumphs and defeats, victories in fits and starts. Certainly the party was stronger in 1990 than it was in 1966, but compared to its neighbors in the southern United States Arkansas remained, and stubbornly so, a strong Democratic state. The "Reagan Revolution" did not transform Arkansas politics. A southern state that had never popularly elected a Republican to the US Senate, never seen a majority of its four US House seats held by Republicans at once, consistently elected supermajorities of Democrats to serve in the state

House and Senate, and remained steadfastly Democratic in most county and local elections, had just seen its Democratic governor of twelve of the last fourteen years elected president. Apart from Rockefeller's time in the governor's mansion, Hammerschmidt's perennial dominance of one US House congressional district, and a smattering of others enjoying relatively short-term tenures in Congress as Republicans in office, the state politics of Arkansas ends this first generation of the modern party in much the same way it began—overwhelmingly Democratic. However, this is the era when the Republican Party of Arkansas shifted from something akin to a third-party organization to a viable component of a two-party system. Thus, one of Rockefeller's stated goals was met. In terms of raw numbers of Republicans in office during this generation, it could be easy to write off the party, were it not the period where the initial, organizational building blocks were laid out, albeit slowly. If not for the advancements made regarding the party gaining relative traction in the state during this period, Republicans would not have been so well poised to seize opportunities in the second iteration of the modern GOP in Arkansas.

The Second Generation: 1992-2010

The second generation of the modern Republican Party of Arkansas, I argue, begins in 1992. However, lacking a specific point in time where Republicans in the state garnered a historic victory (as in 1966, when Winthrop Rockefeller's gubernatorial win marked the beginning of the first-generation era), this next era emerged more gradually, and might be considered by some to have begun in 1990. As I contend later, 1992 marked the beginning, if only by happenstance or the party's good fortune, of the most successful decade in the twentieth century for Arkansas Republicans.

However, 1990, at least in one respect, serves as a key bridge between the first and second generation. Whether it was the sign of growth in appeal of the party among Arkansans or the strategic participation of would-be Democratic voters in the 1990 GOP gubernatorial primary (to ensure that Sheffield Nelson won the nomination, effectively thwarting the populism of Tommy Robinson), the fact was that the nomination contest had garnered a historically high number of votes cast in a GOP primary. The contest had been a bruising affair and risked fracturing the state party, the result of which set the party back further and failed to capitalize on any momentum it hoped to gain the 1990s.[34] In an attempt to heal political wounds within its ranks, Republican Party of Arkansas leaders and activists selected Nelson and Asa Hutchinson to cochair the state party as a gesture of unity. Nelson, of course, had just lost to Bill Clinton after switching his party affiliation from Democratic to Republican and securing the party's nomination for governor. Hutchinson was a lifelong Republican and a rising star of the GOP, who had previously been appointed by President Reagan to serve as the US attorney for the Western District of Arkansas. He had been born and raised in Northwest Arkansas, the only consistently Republican region of the state for years. Nelson would go on to be elected national committeeman of the GOP in 1991, and Hutchinson would continue to serve as state party chair during the eventful early 1990s before his election to the US House of Representatives in 1996.

In 1992, Arkansas would not only witness significant political activity and competition but also draw the attention of national and international political observers. Despite his pledge to serve out the four-year term he had been granted by voters in his 1990 reelection bid, no observer of Arkansas politics was surprised when Clinton announced his intention to seek his party's nomination for president in October 1991. He went on to secure the Democratic nomination and unseated the Republican incumbent, George H. W. Bush, in November 1992. Clinton was a native son of the Natural State, a Rhodes scholar who earned degrees from Georgetown and Yale. He then returned to Arkansas to serve as its attorney general before being elected governor. The story of Clinton's ascendance to the most powerful political position in the world is, in and of itself, appropriately well documented. However, his campaign and eventual victory in 1992, while setting up much of what followed in the state's politics, is outside the scope of this book. In short, Clinton's victory is significant to the eventual taking over of the state's politics by the GOP in the way it created a power vacuum in a state known for its political stability and—up to that point in time—one-party dominance.

In addition to Governor Clinton's bid for the White House, the 1992 election cycle proved impactful in other ways. First, John Paul Hammerschmidt, who had served in the US House of Representatives since 1967—often the lone Republican of the state's congressional members and Arkansas's most prominent GOP official—announced his retirement. The seat remained in Republican hands, with the Third Congressional District being represented by Tim Hutchinson, brother to then-chairman of the Republican Party of Arkansas, Asa Hutchinson. The election cycle would also see a Republican, Jay Dickey, representing the Fourth District, which covered a large portion of southern and western Arkansas. This split the partisan balance of the state's US

House delegation. One US Senate seat, occupied by former Democratic governor Dale Bumpers since 1975, was up for reelection in 1992. Bumpers's Republican opponent was a relatively unknown pastor and media broadcaster from South Arkansas, Mike Huckabee.

Despite losing to Bumpers in 1992, Huckabee's campaign garnered nearly 39 percent of the vote against a popular incumbent.[35] As a result of Clinton's ascendance from the governor's mansion to the White House, Huckabee's campaign for the US Senate would quickly transition to a special election campaign for the office of lieutenant governor. At the time of Clinton's announcement to run for president in 1991, the state constitution required that the lieutenant governor assume the duties of governor when the state executive was out of Arkansas—resulting in recently elected Lieutenant Governor Jim Guy Tucker often serving in place of Clinton, even before formally replacing the outgoing governor in December 1992. Shortly thereafter, Huckabee narrowly defeated Democrat Nate Coulter to fill the open lieutenant governor position in a special election.

While Democrats celebrated their native son's election as president of the United States, and were encouraged that Tucker, a Democrat, former congressman, and attorney general, would serve as governor, Clinton's departure from the state created a political void for Democrats in Arkansas. One of "the Big Three" who had so masterfully managed to persuade Arkansas voters—largely disapproving of the liberal stances of the national Democratic platform—that Arkansas Democrats were still in line with national party's values was now leaving the state. The first element of change in the state's political makeup at this time was Huckabee's victory in the special election for lieutenant governor. His electoral win marked only the second time a Republican had been elected to the office since Reconstruction. A few years later, Senator David Pryor, one of the Big Three Democrats who had served in the US House and as governor before being elected to the Senate in 1978, announced his retirement at the end of his term in January 1997. With Clinton in the White House, and Tucker as governor, a Republican had as good a chance as ever to be elected, for the first time in the history of the state, to the US Senate. Certainly, among Republicans, Lieutenant Governor Huckabee was the odds-on favorite to secure his party's nomination for the contest. However, as Governor Tucker dealt with criminal charges and an eventual conviction in matters related to the vast, yearslong Whitewater investigation, Huckabee decided against running for the Senate in favor of assuming the role of governor in the summer of 1996, following Tucker's resignation.[36]

Huckabee's decision to not run for the Senate must not have been an easy one. Political pundits believed the popular Huckabee would likely win the seat in the US Senate.[37] Instead, he assumed the role of governor midway through Tucker's original term. As for the Senate seat, Tim Hutchinson, who was serving as the US House representative for the Third Congressional District, beat Democratic candidate Winston Bryant and became the first Republican in Arkansas to be elected to the US Senate since the ratification of the Seventeenth Amendment to the Constitution in 1913. Hutchinson's election to the Senate also left a vacancy in what was now a reliably Republican US House district, picked up by his brother and former chair of the Republican Party of Arkansas, Asa Hutchinson.

Regardless of the unconventional way in which he assumed the position, the positive impact of Huckabee's tenure as governor on the Republican Party of Arkansas, which began in 1996, was significant in many ways. In addition to the positive effects a popular gubernatorial incumbent like Huckabee might have on his party—particularly in terms of fundraising and candidate recruitment—Arkansas governors enjoy significant appointment power over state boards and commissions. According to the governor's office, the governor is responsible for the appointment of approximately 350 boards and commissions—ranging from the obscure to some of the most powerful unelected political posts in the state. Governors have long exercised their appointment power to reward loyalists and attempt to broaden their base. However, with exception of both of Rockefeller's two-year terms and White's single two-year term, a Republican governor had not yet been able to capitalize on appointment powers in any significant way politically. Before Huckabee, Republicans had only had three terms (at the time in which Rockefeller and White held office, six years) in a span of over one hundred years to exercise appointment powers in ways that rewarded party loyalists, and—most importantly—cultivated hundreds of potential political talents who might one day run as Republicans in the state. Huckabee's more than ten years as governor meant, among other things, that he would use appointments to boards and commissions to reward the party faithful and, most importantly, cultivate and grant experience to a new generation of Arkansans who were less inclined to be blinded by the state's dominant Democratic history.

The 1990s began with a hotly contested race for the Republican nomination for governor—a race that yielded a record turnout. Then, due to Clinton's election as president, the office of lieutenant governor became vacant and was filled by a dynamic, charismatic Republican who would assume the role of governor three short years later and hold the seat for just over ten years. A decade in which national and regional political winds favored Republicans in southern states, Republicans enjoyed unprecedented—albeit limited by most state politics standards—successes. Wekkin wrote, "The 1990s . . . thus far suggest a new era of Republican growth in Arkansas. Republicans at present control 50 percent of the state's congressional delegation plus the offices of governor and lieutenant governor. And although the Democrats continue to dominate the state legislature, both the number of two-party contests for seats in the Arkansas General Assembly and the size of the Republican vote shares in statewide and legislative races are as high in the 1990s as they were in the Rockefeller years."[38] The decade closed with split congressional seats (two House Republicans and two House Democrats; one Democrat and one Republican in the Senate); a Republican governor; and a Republican lieutenant governor. And—in keeping with what had become tradition (with the exception of Jimmy Carter in 1976 and Clinton in 1992 and 1996)—the state went for Republican George W. Bush in 2000. However, while Huckabee's success certainly moved the state party forward, and his appointment powers helped create, arguably for the first time ever, a "bench" for GOP recruitment, his successes did not immediately result in lasting GOP gains within the state.

Undoubtedly, the GOP in Arkansas ended the 1990s in a considerably stronger position than when the decade began. However, despite an increase in apparent recruitment efforts and numbers of Republicans filing for offices at the state legislative and local levels of government, the GOP still had far to go. As the perennial party out of power for decades, these gains—while significant—might fail to impress an outside observer, as both chambers of the General Assembly remained dominated by Democratic majorities and local offices still advantaged Democrats in most parts of the state. This would not change for another twelve years.

In addition to boasting a Republican governor, lieutenant governor, US Senator, and two members of the US House to begin the twenty-first century, Arkansas Republicans—perhaps for the first time—had reason to believe that the first decade of the new millennium would mark the beginning of their political dominance in much the same way they had seen their party peers succeed in other southern states. To break the cycle of Arkansas being one of the longest-running, most dominant single-party states in the union, Republicans would need consistent gains in vote share. What began to take shape in the 1970s, and became more apparent later in the 1990s and early 2000s, was the gradual movement of Arkansas voters from Democratic supremacy to the Republican ranks. However, this could have been easily lost in the election returns that resulted in the state's six electoral college votes going to Clinton in 1992 and 1996, and continued to send Democrats to Congress and—overwhelmingly—to the General Assembly. While very subtle, the data by the early 2000s indicated a shift in voting behavior. Arkansas voters had long favored Republicans at the top of the ticket (president of the United States, for example) and that support positively impacted GOP candidates down-ticket as well, if at a glacial pace. In their analyses, based on Democratic vote share from 1976 to 2004, Andrew Dowdle and Wekkin illustrated a trend of decreasing support for Democratic candidates—resulting in what they determined was "top-down" Republican growth.[39]

While the overall voter trends were (very) slowly moving in Republicans' favor in Arkansas, the wind was far from being at the backs of most of the party's candidates in the state. Despite the well-founded optimism that must have filled the GOP faithful in 2000, that election cycle would result in one fewer Republican congressman from the state as incumbent Dickey lost to Mike Ross, a Democratic state legislator from Southwest Arkansas. Further illustrating the party's pattern of gains mixed with losses, the 2002 election cycle was an overall disappointment. While Governor Huckabee (by a surprisingly slim margin) and Lieutenant Governor Winthrop Paul Rockefeller were reelected, Republicans made no gains in other state constitutional offices, and lost the US Senate seat won by Tim Hutchinson six years before to the state's attorney general, Mark Pryor—son of the former governor and US Senator David Pryor.[40]

In January 2007, Governor Huckabee had termed out of office. The symbolic and practical political value for the party of having an approachable figure like Huckabee representing the state's highest constitutional office was enormous. A strong candidate to replace him was current lieutenant governor Winthrop Paul Rockefeller. Rockefeller had won the seat in a special election in 1996 after Huckabee ascended to governor. Rockefeller was popular among voters, and garnered more support in his 2002 reelection than Huckabee. Tragically, Rockefeller was diagnosed with myeloproliferative disease, a blood disorder that can develop into leukemia, and dropped out of the race.[41] He would succumb to his illness later that year at the age of fifty-seven.

In addition to Rockefeller announcing his run for governor prior to his diagnosis, Asa Hutchinson had indicated his intention to seek the GOP nomination in 2006. Prior to resigning to run for governor, Hutchinson had served as undersecretary for the newly created Department of Homeland Security.[42] Rockefeller's dropping out of the race left the nomination unopposed for Hutchinson, who had previously served as a federal prosecutor, Arkansas Republican Party chair, and member of the US House of Representatives. The Democratic nominee whom Hutchinson would have to defeat in 2006 to keep the governorship in Republican hands was the state's attorney general and former state senator Mike Beebe.

The 2006 election results seemed to indicate a state reverting back to its traditional Democratic ways. Following Election Day, all constitutional offices—including governor, both US Senate seats, three of the state's four US House seats, and sizeable majorities in both chambers of the General Assembly—would be held by Democrats, a major setback for the GOP in the state. Two years later would be much like 2006, with Republicans failing to even recruit a candidate to face Pryor in his reelection bid for the US Senate—a seat previously held by Tim Hutchinson before his defeat to Pryor in 2002. Despite over ten years with Huckabee as governor and Arkansans consistently favoring Republican presidential candidates, the party—as a brand and organizational structure in 2008—had not been so weak in decades. Recalling the state of the party at the time, Doyle Webb, chairman of the Arkansas Republican Party from 2009 to 2020, expressed both the frustrations and optimism at the closing of the second generation of the party when he said, "2009 was a difficult year for us. We had trouble fundraising and recruiting candidates, but we could see things happening."[43]

Though the period ended on a less than promising note, the second generation of the party—spanning nearly twenty years—brought unprecedented successes. However, despite the historical nature of their accomplishments, the gains by the GOP in the state during this time were still relatively modest. The era saw one Republican governor who served in the role for more than two terms and had the potential to have an arguably greater impact than any other state Republican of the era. With the election of Tim Hutchinson, the state had selected a Republican US Senator by popular vote for the first time in history. Also during this time, Republicans showed they could not only compete in US House races, but also win on occasion. Finally, the party appeared to be competitive in state legislative races, albeit in fits and starts and still resulting in the party's perennial minority status largely based in Northwest Arkansas.

This is a common theme throughout the first and second generations of the modern Republican Party in Arkansas—whether by Republican dynamism or Democratic misstep, the GOP, prior to 2010, enjoyed occasional moments of electoral success, only to fail at gaining the type of momentum a party needs to capitalize on fledgling transformational partisan change among an electorate.

The Third Generation—2010s to Today

The third generation begins in 2010 and continues today. Despite significant gains in all other southern states, Republicans in the late 2000s found a Democratic firewall in Arkansas—particularly in down-ticket election contests. While Arkansas voters continued to strengthen their collective preference for Republican presidential candidates—granting the state's six electoral college votes to Republicans in all but three elections between 1972 and 2008, Democrats continued to dominate in the state. There were noteworthy exceptions, however. Mike Huckabee, a Republican, served the state as governor from 1996 to 2007, and the state sent its first-ever popularly elected Republican to the US Senate in in 1997, Tim Hutchinson. However, Democrats continued to maintain significant majorities in both state legislative chambers, normally held all other state constitutional positions, and typically could claim at least half of the state's US congressional delegation until the end of the first decade of the new millennium. However, beginning in 2010, things began to dramatically change as Republicans made historic gains in the state—going from perennial underdog to dominating Arkansas politics in just under four years, or two election cycles.

It is difficult to express the stark contrast between the close of the second generation to start of the third stage of the modern GOP in Arkansas. Despite considerable gains in the 1990s, and Republicans in the state benefiting from the popularity of President George W. Bush among Arkansas voters, much of the momentum from that era had dissipated over the first decade of the century.[44] By 2008, Democratic governor Mike Beebe enjoyed popularity among Arkansans—as he worked with a Democratic-controlled General Assembly. The state's US Senators were both Democrats (one of whom, Mark Pryor, would not even face a Republican opponent in 2008), and three of the four US House of Representatives were also Democrats.

The third generation begins in 2010, as Republicans in Arkansas and many other states that cycle saw an increase in mobilization and electoral competition—whether inspired by the economic recession, the election of President Barack Obama, or the Tea Party movement. In 2010, Beebe and one of three Democratic incumbent US House members, Mike Ross, were reelected. Governor Beebe secured reelection by winning the majority of votes in all of the state's seventy-five counties. However, for the rest of the slate of Democratic incumbents, 2010 was an entirely different story. The state's Second Congressional District incumbent, Democrat Vic Snyder, announced his retirement in 2009, leaving the contest to a matchup between Tim Griffin, a former US district attorney and member of the Bush administration, and Joyce Elliott, Democratic majority leader of the state senate. Griffin would win the Central Arkansas seat. In Eastern Arkansas, another Democratic incumbent, Marion Berry, had announced his retirement. Political newcomer Rick Crawford, a Republican, defeated Berry's former chief of staff Chad Causey. The Third District, at this point a decades-old stronghold for the GOP, was retained by Steve Womack. In the race for US senator, Republican John Boozman unseated the Democratic incumbent, Blanche Lincoln. Additionally, Republicans won over two-thirds of all state House seats and all state Senate seats contested in 2010.[45] The 2010 cycle may have seemed to usher in a new level of Republican success in Arkansas, but it was the 2012 and 2014 cycles that solidified GOP dominance in the state as the party not only gained all state constitutional offices, but also the remaining US Senate and US House seat, and majorities in both chambers of the state's General Assembly. The GOP in Arkansas, in the midst of the third generation of the party's modern history, finds itself firmly established as the dominant party, enjoying the highest level of party identification among Arkansas voters in state polling history, along with often substantial fundraising advantages over their opponents.[46]

When defining the three generations, I have considered significant electoral events as markers along the decades-long stretch of time encompassing the modern GOP in Arkansas. To me, the first generation clearly begins in 1966 with Rockefeller's and Hammerschmidt's elections. However, other researchers might reasonably contend that the era begins two years earlier, upon Rockefeller's first unsuccessful gubernatorial campaign. Regardless, the historical impact of Rockefeller's 1966 victory is obvious and Hammerschmidt winning his congressional seat secured the Third District for Republicans for decades thereafter and even today. The start date for the second generation is less obvious. Instead of placing its beginning on a key election or several Republican victories in one cycle, I have assigned it a year when the state's Democratic governor defeated a Republican incumbent for president of the United States. Why? Because, without Clinton's move to the White House, we would not have seen the political vacuum created by his absence for at least another election cycle or two, and Arkansas may have had a Senator Huckabee in 1996—a big step for Republicans, but likely denying a Republican in the governor's mansion for another decade or two, where state-centric policymaking and candidate recruitment were more likely to have occurred to benefit the future of the party. Of course, nobody could have anticipated Tucker's 1996 resignation and Huckabee's ascendance to governor in the fall of 1992, or the resulting special election for lieutenant governor in the spring of 1993, but these things couldn't have happened—at least in this sequence—without Clinton resigning to assume the office of president. The beginning of the third generation is obvious, and the primary impetus for this book. The first generation begins in 1966 and ends in 1991. The second ends at the close of the first decade of the twenty-first century. The fact that Arkansas remained a stubbornly Democratic state well into the latter part of the twentieth century and even into the 2000s was, in part, what made Arkansas stand out from its regional peers and neighbors. In other words, the third generation, which began in 2010, might not have been defined at all if, like many other southern states, Arkansas had become steadily more Republican during the 1990s. If things would have worked the way many at the time might have reasonably assumed, 1994 might have been the most sensible time to anticipate the first generation of GOP dominance in the state. But despite electing and reelecting Governor Huckabee, Arkansas remained exceptional among its southern neighbors by staying largely Democratic.

The third generation, in which we find ourselves today, presents a dramatically different landscape, as the party not only gained offices but also increased their presence in all levels of federal, state, and local government. The state's electorate has realigned its partisan loyalties to heavily advantage the GOP and secure its dominance for the foreseeable future. The rise of the Republican Party in Arkansas cannot be explained by a single factor. Rather, several factors converged to create the current political and partisan climate in Arkansas that we see today. With this chapter, I have organized the development of the modern Republican Party in Arkansas into three generations. Each generation is unique in both the political and electoral status of the party and the amount of power the party possessed in the politics and policy of the state over a given period.

Moving forward, I will pay particular attention to the overlap between the end of the second generation and the beginning of the third generation. The following chapters will further analyze the party's rise from being one of the weakest, least effective major party organizations in the United States to enjoying electoral dominance in almost every aspect of Arkansas politics. This transformation, as I have suggested, did not occur overnight—even if the party's rise might have seemed an overnight phenomenon. This chapter has chronicled—in short order—the better part of six decades but has not analyzed the multiple factors leading up to the rise of the GOP in the Natural State. I've organized my analysis in the following chapters according to V. O. Key's "tripartite of party"—examining the Republican Party of Arkansas as it relates to the state's electorate, the state party's organization, and state governance.

3

THE CHANGING ARKANSAS ELECTORATE AND THE RISE OF THE GOP IN ARKANSAS

The Arkansas electorate has heavily favored Republican candidates over the last decade. While the electoral gains for Republicans in Arkansas seemed to appear overnight, a deeper analysis provides considerably more nuance. The state's moderate to conservative populist leanings are not new, and one could be forgiven for assuming the state's GOP has enjoyed success at this current scale for at least a few decades instead of a few years. However, as observers of Arkansas politics know, this shift in voting behavior was remarkable in its abruptness. Furthermore, to an outside observer it might be difficult to believe that Arkansans consistently and overwhelmingly elected Democratic candidates for generations—with such loyalty to those running under the party banner that Arkansas was known as one of the most Democratic states in the country.[1] On the other hand, Arkansans were also known to have an independent streak and a lack of attachment (harboring on disdain) to liberal national Democratic Party politics—all the while electing Democrats, cycle after cycle.

The story of the Arkansas voter, particularly since the 1960s, is multidimensional. Since 1972, Arkansans favored the Republican candidate for president of the United States unless the Democratic candidate was a southerner (in the case of Jimmy Carter in 1976) or a native of the Natural State (Bill Clinton in 1992 and again in 1996). In short, election results could overstate and oversimplify the breadth and depth of party loyalty among the state's electorate. Despite this, Democratic Party candidates dominated Arkansas politics—even after its southern neighbors shed their long-held post–Civil War allegiances to the regionalized and often rebellious southern Democratic brand.

We are only a handful of election cycles into an era of Republican dominance of Arkansas politics and the precipitous decline of the Democrats in the state. The focus of this chapter is on the party in the electorate—in this case, partisan politics and Arkansas voters. What led to the dramatic shift in voting behavior—and eventually, partisan leanings—in Arkansas? This chapter is organized into the three generations of the modern Republican Party of Arkansas in order to analyze the voting behavior of the Arkansas electorate over time and explain the root causes of the shift to the partisan voter loyalty we see today.

As outlined, 1966 begins the first generation of the modern Republican Party in Arkansas. The year is significant, as it marked the election of the first Republican governor of Arkansas in the twentieth century and the election of a Republican member of the US House of Representatives in the northwestern region of the state—a seat that has remained Republican ever since. The second half of the 1960s also marked the passage of the Civil Rights Act of 1964. Consequently, the decade saw the beginning of GOP electoral gains in the South. The end of the era of post-Reconstruction Democratic dominance in many southern states is marked by this period. It also marks beginning of an era of phasing out the Republican Party's coalition of whites and Blacks in Arkansas. Boris Heersink and Jeffrey Jenkins explain that, unlike many other southern states, the post–Civil War Republican Party in Arkansas was long comprised of a biracial coalition of whites and Blacks, despite challenges to Black voter participation and occasional waves of "Lily-White" party leaders who sought to exclude African Americans from the party.[2] According to Heersink and Jenkins, "This cooperation between white and black Republicans continued through the 1930s and into the 1940s, even as blacks in Arkansas began to move wholesale into the Democratic Party. By the early 1950s, the Republican Party in Arkansas, while Lily-White in name, remained a biracial coalition."[3] Apart from the historic significance of Winthrop Rockefeller's election in 1966 and reelection two years later, his political peak of popularity came at a point of transition for the Republican Party in the United States. Speaking of Rockefeller, his coalition of supporters, the progressivism his tenure as governor inspired, and his impact in the state's political history, journalist and historian Rex Nelson said:

> He saved us as a state while we saved him as an individual. And by that, I mean, he forced a new progressive era in Arkansas politics. And we saved him because we really gave him purpose in life, which he was struggling [with] when he moved here. That's why he got away from the Manhattan social scene and moved to Arkansas. But Rockefeller, of course, had gotten elected by getting large majorities of the African American vote in Arkansas by bringing in moderate to "we're just ready for an end to the segregationists" era of Democratic politics. The Democrats, of course, do nominate a segregationist in Jim Johnson in '66. They come back in '68 with Marian Crank, who is also a member of the so-called old guard of the Arkansas Democratic Party. And by '70, I think Democratic primary voters had said, "Look, we've got to make a change." Faubus, of course, had come back after four years out of office, decided to run, and in '70 thought he would waltz back into office, but voters had changed by then and Dale Bumpers was something fresh—he was something different. But I firmly believe without a Winthrop Rockefeller for those four years, a Dale Bumpers never would have been possible. David Pryor never would have been possible. Thus, a Bill Clinton never would have been possible. So because of Rockefeller defeating the Democratic nominee in '66 and '68, it forced the majority party to change. And when the majority party changed, the Republican Party had been a party of change. They were kind of left without a place to go for a long time.[4]

At this time, the GOP began to move to a more consistently conservative ideological view. Rockefeller's style of Republicanism was most similar to the reform-minded liberals who then served in the northeastern United States, not the stridently conservative politics associated with Barry Goldwater and Ronald Reagan. These architects of the new wave of Republicans would usher in a modern era for a party poised to gain ground in most southern states in the decades to follow. In short, Rockefeller's rise in Arkansas was a movement that was his and his alone—as his party meanwhile sought to move to a more consistently conservative policy position. In addition to the ideological differences emerging between Rockefeller and his party, this split stemming from Rockefeller's two terms as governor was further complicated by the lack of a formal party organizational structure—a topic explored in the next chapter.

For well over a century, general election results were essentially a mere formality, as most Arkansas voters routinely selected among a field of Democratic nominees for partisan elected office, establishing the winners months prior in the primary. The 1966 general election brought forth a glimpse into the future of the Arkansas electorate, however, as Arkansans elected Republican governor Rockefeller and US House representative John Paul Hammerschmidt—Arkansas firsts, in both cases, since Reconstruction. Arkansans' ability to illustrate a streak of unpredictability—albeit rare in occurrence—was even more apparent in 1968, when they reelected Rockefeller and Hammerschmidt, retained Vietnam War critic and Democrat J. William Fulbright in the US Senate, and favored race-baiting former governor of Alabama George Wallace for president. Regarding the 1968 results, Jim Ranchino wrote: "Some accused Arkansans of going to the polls blindfolded; others were less kind and described the response as political schizophrenia. At least three scholars of national reputation took one look at the precinct returns in the official records of the Secretary of State's Office in Little Rock and walked away with a dull headache and an unbelievable shake of the head. The results simply made no sense."[5]

Despite the perplexing results of 1968, one thing begins to crystalize during this period: Arkansas voters had begun to move away from Democratic presidential candidates in the 1960s and developed a negative association with the national Democratic brand—and its more liberal policy agenda, which began to diminish their century-long loyalty to the Democratic Party. In his profile of a typical "Arkansas voter" during this period, Ranchino stated: "If you had to describe the 'average' Arkansas voter in detail, the voter who actually participates regularly in the democratic process (which is only about 32 percent of those of voting age), it would go something like this. The voter is white, male, Baptist, about forty-nine years of age.... He considers himself a Democrat, and usually votes for the party's nominees, although his party loyalties are less than deep, especially at the national level."[6]

Ranchino, being an astute observer of Arkansas politics in the 1960s and early 1970s, had also surveyed Arkansas voters and found that, despite the growing independent streak apparent in the voting behavior of the state's electorate, a majority of voters still identified as a Democrat (59 percent) while only 17 percent claimed to be Republican.

To summarize these survey results, he wrote, "In everyday terms these percentages proclaim clearly that if a Republican wins a state-wide race, Democrats elect him by providing the essential majority."[7] This proved to be the case in 1966 and again in 1968 when Rockefeller was elected and reelected as governor, and again in 1972 when an overwhelming majority of voters supported President Nixon's landslide reelection. Arkansans began a trend that has continued well into the twenty-first century, in which a majority of the state's votes for president go for the Republican candidate (unless the Democrat was southern, as was the case in 1976, 1992, and 1996). Arkansas reverted into the Democratic column for Carter in 1976—supporting a southern Democratic candidate—only to revert back to the Republicans in 1980 by narrowly favoring Reagan's bid over the incumbent Carter. While still overwhelmingly Democratic in most down-ballot contests, Arkansas chose Reagan and George H. W. Bush in 1984 and 1988, respectively. In 1992 and 1996, Arkansas supported their Democratic governor, Bill Clinton, in his campaign for the presidency and in his subsequent successful reelection bid. From that point on, Arkansans have exclusively favored Republican candidates for president, as growing numbers of Arkansans rejected the more liberal national Democratic Party brand.

This view of an "out of touch" Democratic Party was slow to develop in any meaningful way, as Democrats in Arkansas continued to win most statewide and local contests in the 1990s and 2000s. However, by 1990, Republicans had begun to see the potential of associating the national Democratic image with that of the state's elected Democrats as a means to pick up voters who already favored Republicans at the top of the ticket.

In 1990, Governor Clinton, who had served from 1979–81 and again since 1983, had concluded his first four-year term of office (as voters had approved a constitutional amendment in 1984 that extended two-year terms to four years). Over the second half of the 1980s, Clinton had increased his presence in national Democratic circles by positioning himself as a centrist problem solver who worked outside of his national party's more liberal ideals. By 1988, as outgoing chair of the National Governors Association, he was considered a potential candidate for president and spoke at a prominent time slot of the Democratic National Convention that year. Though he did not choose to run for national office in 1988, there was considerable speculation that he would, in fact, seek his party's nomination for president in 1992. This speculation complicated his reelection bid in 1990. If reelected, would he carry out the full, four-year term as governor? Would he be focused on Arkansans, or his own progressive political ambitions? Meanwhile, Republican voters faced—arguably for the first time ever—two politically prominent and electorally viable gubernatorial candidates competing for the Republican nomination that year: Tommy Robinson and Sheffield Nelson.

Robinson was a former sheriff of Pulaski County, the state's most populous county, and he was the current member of the US House of Representatives for Arkansas's Second District—which included the state's capital city, Little Rock, and other communities in Central Arkansas. First elected to the US House in 1984 as a Democrat, he made national headlines when he announced that he was switching parties in the summer of 1989. The announcement was a spectacle of sorts, as it was made at an official press briefing of President Bush. During the press conference, Robinson explained his move by suggesting the party he had represented in two congressional cycles in the 1980s now left him with what he perceived to be policy positions that were out of touch with Arkansan values. He went on to compare himself and his party loyalties to that of President Harry Truman, calling himself a "lunch-bucket Democrat," but, he said:

> Today, to best serve the people of Arkansas and to stay true to the values of my family and an ever-increasing number of Arkansans, I could no longer be a member of the national Democratic Party. This is a very personal private decision. It has been long in coming because frankly, I hoped that the national Democratic Party would come back home and once again be in touch with the mainstream of the American people, but even after losing five of the last six presidential elections both nationwide and in Arkansas the leadership of the national Democratic Party still is unwilling to listen to the majority of the American people.[8]

Earlier that year, Robinson had colorfully attempted to draw distinctions between Democrats in his state and the national party: "The Arkansas Democrat is nothing like the national Democrat. They're hard-working people, they believe in God and motherhood and chivalry and apple pie, and the eastern liberals have pointy heads and they carry big briefcases around with nothing inside them but ham sandwiches."[9]

It is now known that Lee Atwater, Republican strategist and chairman of the Republican National Committee from 1989 until 1991, had sought out Robinson as a strong opponent to Clinton, who Atwater anticipated would run for president in 1992.[10] Robinson's strong personality and populist appeal made him a formidable foe to the forty-three-year-old Clinton, who, despite his young age and national appeal, was already one of the state's longest serving governors and may have lacked the same voter excitement he might have enjoyed in earlier election cycles. Arkansas's open partisan primaries also meant that Robinson was clearly catering to those growing numbers of Arkansas voters who, despite identifying as Democrats or independents, had begun to vote for Republican presidential candidates in the 1970s and were now voting for Republicans down-ticket as well.

Despite the press attention and enormous shot in the arm for his gubernatorial bid by President Bush, Robinson had to face another prominent former Democrat turned Republican for the GOP nomination— Sheffield Nelson—if he was to compete against Clinton in the general election. Nelson had been a prominent figure in Arkansas business for years but was a first-time candidate for office. While Robinson's party switch was expected to draw support from the state's more populist conservatives, Nelson's joining the Republican Party was celebrated by longtime Republican officials in the state, who were labeled by Robinson as "the country club crowd."[11] In describing the strange nature of these two political combatants who, while quite different in nearly every measure, shared a strong history with the Democratic Party, David Broder wrote, "As if the spring floods were not enough, nice old conservative Arkansas finds itself facing a Tuesday gubernatorial primary between a man who contributed $1,000 to Edward M. Kennedy's 1980 presidential campaign and one who voted for Jesse L. Jackson at the 1988 Democratic convention. And those are the Republicans." While most of the focus was on the two Republicans competing for their party's nomination for governor that year, Clinton also faced an opponent, Tom McRae IV, the grandson of a former Arkansas governor and long-time head of the Winthrop Rockefeller Foundation. In the same piece, Broder summed up the nature of the GOP primary and Clinton's own intraparty contest against McRae when he wrote, "This election has a Kurt Vonnegut script and a 'Saturday Night Live' director."

In the weeks leading up to the primary elections, the chairman of the Democratic Party of Arkansas, Skip Rutherford, encouraged fellow Democrats to vote in the Republican primary for governor and select Nelson, in order to take votes away from Robinson, who was seen as the bigger threat to Clinton in the fall. Rutherford's call to action was repeated by longtime journalist John Brummett in a series of pieces from his opinion column.[12] While it may be impossible to measure the exact impact made by otherwise-Democratic voters who sought to "spoil" the GOP primary, voters cast more than three times the number of votes than in the 1986 GOP presidential primary—suggesting historically high interest in the gubernatorial primary contest. Nelson ultimately bested Robinson by just over eight thousand votes. On the Democratic side, Clinton won his primary with an uninspired 54 percent of the vote against McRae.

Table 3.1
Presidential Election Winner in Arkansas by Year, 1968-92

Year	Candidate	Party
1968	Wallace	American Independent
1972	Nixon*	Republican
1976	Carter*	Democratic
1980	Reagan*	Republican
1984	Reagan*	Republican
1988	Bush*	Republican
1992	Clinton*	Democratic

Note: * denotes the winner of Arkansas's Electoral College votes who also won the presidential election.

Despite the apparent popularity in the state for Republican presidential candidates, this new GOP affinity was largely isolated to the top of the ticket until the 1990s. Further, while Arkansans seemed predestined to reject the more liberal policy positions of the national Democratic Party, elected officials in Arkansas—the Big Three in particular—managed to effectively negotiate positions and be seen as independent of the national party brand while also being very familiar to their in-state constituencies.

The charisma and political intelligence shared by Bumpers, Pryor, and Clinton allowed the Democratic brand to withstand the tribulations of Democrats in neighboring southern states for quite some time, where politics had become more nationalized, less locally focused, and more polarized. Bumpers, Pryor, and Clinton—along with others seeking to thread themselves within the patchwork of the state's Democratic history while also offering their own unique brand of progressivism and pragmatism distinct from the largely unpopular national party brand's liberalism—served in elected office from the 1960s into the twenty-first century. Bumpers and Pryor represented Arkansas through the 1980s and most of the 1990s in the US Senate, while Clinton served as president from 1993 to 2001. Despite effective appeals to Arkansas voters in presidential elections—specifically, white conservatives—beginning in the 1960s, Republicans struggled to effectively convince the same Natural State voters that the GOP candidates down-ticket would also be to their liking. It seems the brand of Democratic politics ascribed to the Big Three (particularly to Clinton, who ascended from the governor's mansion to the White House) had mitigated Republican successes in the state in favor of a brand of partisan politics and policy that was, apparently, a better fit for Arkansans—specifically, conservative white Arkansans. Who better, among the Democrats, to combat an image of an out-of-step, too-liberal party than an Arkansas favorite son who, as president, was the most prominent Democrat in the country? Capturing the politics of Arkansas at the time, Jay Barth, Diane Blair, and Ernest Dumas wrote: "Arkansas politics in the 1990s has been both a throwback to the past and window to the future. Reminiscent of traditional southern politics, election alliances and outcomes were often influenced by intense personal rivalries with regard to the increasing acceptability—though until 1996 still-infrequent occurrence—of Republican victories, new partisan political patterns were clearly unfolding. Overshadowing and affecting everything else that occurred in Arkansas politics in the 1990s, however, was the historic election and reelection of a native son, Bill Clinton, as president."[13]

Despite the limited success of their candidates, illustrating the GOP brand as consistently conservative to attract ticket-splitting voters in Arkansas was a focus of the state party during this time. On these efforts, former chairman of the Republican Party of Arkansas Asa Hutchinson said:

> We used the media a lot. Sheriff Marlin Hawkins wrote a book that came out during that time, [called] *How I Stole Elections*. I'd been talking about the "Democrat machine" in Arkansas, and I went and held a news conference holding up his book: "See, there's proof they have been stealing elections in Arkansas." We were very visible—and very confrontational—because we wanted to show the differences between the parties.[14]

However, these efforts to unite the brand of the national Republican candidates with the state and local GOP proved to be a difficult task. Hutchinson went on to say: "At the national elections, [like the] presidential [race], Arkansas voters identified with the Republican philosophy, and they would vote [for Republican candidates] because there was generally a clear contrast. But it was by tradition, habit, and social engagement that they would vote Democrat locally."[15]

While the 1990s were another decade largely dominated by Democrats in Arkansas, Republicans saw reasons for optimism and growth moving into the new millennium. As Rex Nelson said, "The irony of the early '90s and mid-'90s is the fact that those doors all open for the Republican Party due to things that happened on the Democratic side of the spectrum."[16]

Regarding Clinton's presidential election and the increased number of open seat elections in the 1990s, Hutchinson recalled:

> The talent pool in the Democratic Party was deep in the early '90s. And a lot of people were waiting for Clinton to leave so that they could have an opportunity to be governor or . . . have a shuffling of the offices so their talent pool could . . . run. With Clinton finally going to the White House, that freed up a number of positions. Of course, Jim Guy Tucker became governor. When that turned sour, it gave an opportunity for the lieutenant governor, Mike Huckabee, to succeed him. And that's what we had to have—we had to have open seats so you could compete on an even keel with the other side. We didn't fare well in the '90s running against incumbents. It was still tough, [the] power of incumbency, but with an open seat in a fair playing field, we could compete.[17]

Another significant event occurred during this time that addressed the issue of primary ballot access in Arkansas—a legal challenge would aid in the Republican Party's efforts to recruit candidates to run for local elections and make it possible for more voters to participate in the GOP primaries. According to Hutchinson, who served as chair of the Republican Party of Arkansas during the time of the legal challenge to the state's primary voting laws:

> We had to make structural changes. The primary elections and polling boxes were funded by the parties, and by the candidate's filing fees. So obviously, if you don't have very many candidates paying filing fees, you don't have very much money to put on a primary in the county. The Democrats had a gargantuan amount of money. So in Arkansas County, they would have thirty polling places where you could go vote as a Democrat, while the Republican Party had one. And they would make jokes that you'd have to travel thirty miles be lucky to find it if you're trying to vote in a Republican primary. And of course,

they steered people away from voting [in the] Republican primary as well. So we naturally had very low turnout, and then that fed into the difficulty of recruiting candidates, because look, why would I want to [run as a Republican], nobody votes in the primary. So I filed a constitutional case, saying that under the equal protection clause of our US Constitution we have an unfair election system in Arkansas that does not give equal opportunity for voters of both parties. We lost that at the district court level, and we appealed to the Eighth Circuit Court of Appeals. And they ruled in our favor. And while I thought I was right, I was still a little bit surprised but thrilled with that result. And it was then-senator Beebe that said, "We've got to fix that." And they immediately introduced legislation that said, "Let's not have the parties pay for this. The state should pay for this. And we'll have joint primaries everywhere." That changed things dramatically. So [now] in Arkansas County or Desha County, you had equal opportunity for [both Republicans and Democrats to vote]. Winning that case and having joint primaries publicly funded changed the landscape of our party in Arkansas.[18]

In *Republican Party of Arkansas v. Faulkner County Arkansas* (1995), the Eighth Circuit Court of Appeals ruled that the practice of partisan-funded primaries were a violation of the Fourteenth Amendment of the US Constitution, resulting in state-funded primaries and polling sites—a significant leveling of the playing field for the GOP. In a state with open primaries, this signaled the end of an era when virtually all races were settled in the Democratic primaries as a means of practical necessity. While this was an incredible change in the way primaries were conducted in the state, impacting the key mechanism by which the electorate exercises its will, it would not be until 2014 that more Arkansans would select a GOP primary ballot over a Democratic one.

By the 1990s, Arkansas voters showed they could vote for Republicans—particularly when a contest did not include a Democratic incumbent. However, even as Huckabee, only the third Republican governor since Reconstruction, succeeded his predecessor and was then elected and reelected on his own merit, Democrats still maintained significant majorities in most other elected offices in the state, from other state Constitutional offices and the General Assembly to local positions at the county and city levels. It seemed that Huckabee's electoral success had not translated to lower-ticket races in part because Arkansas swing voters—the same group within the electorate that would vote for a Republican presidential candidate, but support Democrats down-ticket—failed to identify their support for Huckabee as support for his party.

By the late 1990s, Huckabee's own personal brand and electoral organization appears to have dwarfed the GOP state organization. Rex Nelson recalled:

> I left my job as political editor of the *Arkansas Democrat Gazette*, joining Governor Huckabee as his policy and communications director on the day he took office, July 15, and then took a leave from state government to be his campaign manager in 1998. But I can tell you, even by that point in 1998, the Huckabee organization ... was stronger than the Arkansas Republican Party. I remember, [while I was] campaign manager, Richard Bearden was the executive director of the Republican Party of Arkansas at the time. And every Friday, all the campaign managers for the statewide campaigns would get together. And they were really ripping at our coattails. Boozman, who was running for the US Senate at that time, and Betty Dickey, who was running as a Republican for attorney general, wanted us to help them. But I can tell you now, in retrospect, we really couldn't do that ... my only job was to look out for Mike Huckabee and get as much [of the vote], I was shooting for 60 percent. I could not afford to use our campaign to help [Boozman and Dickey] because our polling at the time ... showed there were a lot of "Huckabee / Blanche Lambert Lincoln for Senate / Mark Pryor for attorney general" voters that year, and I couldn't afford to alienate them.[19]

The positive electoral impact of Huckabee's tenure as governor on the Republican Party of Arkansas was significant in many ways. Beyond the expected positive effects a popular gubernatorial incumbent like Huckabee might have upon his political party—particularly in terms of fundraising and candidate recruitment—Arkansas governors enjoy significant appointment power to state boards and commissions. The governor of Arkansas is responsible for the appointment of approximately 350 boards and commissions, ranging from the obscure to some of the most powerful unelected political posts in the state.

According to Governor Huckabee himself, his biggest contribution to the future of the GOP

> was being there long enough to appoint every single person to every board agency and commission. You have to serve just over ten years to do that, because the longest boards are the University of Arkansas board,

the highway commission—those are both ten years—the fish and game commission and the state police are seven years. And then most of them are anywhere from four to six. But unless you can stay in office, and most governors will only be there eight years, so they'll never have the entire highway commission or the entire UA board. Being part of a Republican administration over an extended period of time gave people this comfort that Republicans weren't crazy.[20]

When asked about the political advantages of Huckabee's tenure and political appointments, former governor Mike Beebe—who was elected at the end of Huckabee's second full term—stated:

> I don't remember the number, but with three or four hundred different annual appointments to different boards and commissions, it's pretty staggering how quickly you can begin to change the composition of those [organizations]. . . . You appoint not only people that you think are competent to do it, but also people that share your vision, your philosophy, and your political ambitions. It's naive to think that you don't appoint people that are members of your party or that share your values. And over the course of ten years, [Huckabee] was able to be very influential in putting people into spots that reflected not just his vision, but also loyalty to the Republican Party. You saw that a lot. Now, having said that, a lot of the best ones are apolitical, many of whom I retained. But to his credit, he also retained some that had previously been there, particularly in areas where it's a professional or vocational area of jurisdiction—the soybean board [for instance]. You're going to select the farmers that are involved in that industry and know it—regardless of their political affiliation—and a lot of times those people transcend administrations and transcend political party changes. And that was true with Huckabee as well as with me.[21]

Huckabee's ability to serve more than ten years in office and thus fill every board or commission assignment created a GOP political bench. Before Huckabee, Republicans had only had three terms (or six years total, the combined time in which Rockefeller and White held office) in over one hundred years to exercise appointment powers in ways that rewarded party loyalists, and—most importantly—cultivated hundreds of potential political talents who might one day run as Republican in the state. Huckabee's time as governor meant, among other things, that his appointment power helped his party by creating opportunities for the association of Republicans with politically appointed public service to a new generation of Arkansans less inclined to be blinded by the state's dominant Democratic history.

Hutchinson's efforts and Huckabee's time as governor did not immediately translate to lower-ticket success for the GOP. At this time, Arkansas voters still largely favored Democrats. However, Hutchinson and Huckabee together helped plant the seeds in the 1990s and early 2000s that bore fruit in the third generation of the party in Arkansas. By 2010, the national and state political environment would dramatically change, and the GOP in Arkansas would be poised to not only capitalize on the moment's political winds, but also benefit from a dramatic shift in voting behavior among Arkansans that would endure.

President Obama and the Nationalization of Arkansas Politics

While it might have been difficult to see immediately following the 2008 general election, the GOP was poised to gain significant ground in Arkansas but lacked a catalyst to spark the partisan change that many neighboring states had undergone. The election of President Obama that year and the passage of the Affordable Care Act led to enormous backlash in Arkansas. While it was well established by this point that a majority of Arkansas voters often preferred GOP presidential candidates, the visceral dislike for Obama and his policies from large portions of Arkansans spilled over into the down-ticket races in 2010 and onward. In a PBS story in 2014, Roby Brock, host of a popular business and politics television show who also conducts regular political polls in Arkansas, was quoted as saying that Obama had been "toxic for Arkansas Democrats," that "there [was] a cultural disconnect," and that his unpopularity in the state had been "exploited expertly by Arkansas Republicans."[22] Brock's comments captured the visceral dislike of President Obama, particularly among those voters who had previously voted for Republicans for president, but chose Democrats further down the ballot.

The parochial, personality-based, "retail politics" that seemed to benefit popular, personable Democratic incumbents were coming to an end as the distinction between national and state politics began to blur in the state. On the effects of the nationalization of the state's politics, longtime GOP political consultant Bill Vickery said:

> Since 2010, three things in particular have impacted Arkansas politics. . . . One, the rise of the influence of cable television . . . like

MSNBC, CNN, Fox News, specifically Fox News and what Roger Ailes set out to do there.... That began to dominate the conversation of what was going on in American politics, and specifically in Arkansas politics. I also think the rise of interconnectivity through social media (and through the internet in general) had an enormous amount to do with it, because for the first time big blocks of people could communicate in a decentralized fashion with one another and understand what was going on. Most Arkansans didn't pay attention to cloture votes in the United States Senate, but they sure did in 2010. Because that was a big issue, and Blanche Lincoln lost her US Senate seat because they paid attention not to the actual vote on the floor, but to the cloture vote that allowed [the Affordable Care Act] to be brought to the floor to begin with. How do you know anything about that if you're not ... a political insider? But framed by cable news and distributed by social media a lot of folks [are sharing stories and opinions]. And then lastly, I think the presidency of Barack Obama really brought to bear the schism that had occurred between the conservative Arkansas voter and how their members were being forced to vote on a national level. You had an administration and a president that favored big city urban politics, and [Arkansas voters] felt disenfranchised; they didn't understand why Blanche Lincoln would support this or Mark Pryor would support [that]. Obama forced the hand of a lot of folks to vote on legislation ... that they normally wouldn't [support] in the Senate.[23]

While the extent to which President Obama's race played a factor in the negative reactions among portions of white Americans, including many of those in Arkansas, can be debated, it is well documented that there was a strong relationship between voters' race, attitudes toward people of other races, and their support (or lack thereof) of Obama—particularly in the South.[24] It is also worth noting that in Arkansas some of the most dramatic shifts in voting behavior to benefit Republicans during Obama's presidency took place in the state's whitest counties.[25] However, it is virtually impossible to determine the extent to which Obama's race alone played a role in the political misfortunes of Democrats in Arkansas and the successes of the GOP in the last ten or more years. That is not to say there were not some white Arkansans—motivated by their own racial biases and inflamed at the thought of an African American man in the White House—who altered their voting behaviors or became activated as a voter for the first time, but this group of voters was not alone responsible for the sustained growth of the GOP or demise of the Democratic

Party in the state's current politics. Considering this issue, Nelson posits that, while race may have been a factor for some who disliked Obama, this antagonism alone does not explain why other Democrats—during and after President Obama's two terms in the White House—failed to gain traction among the public in the 2010s and early 2020s: "And then you do have the Obama election as president and I think some of it is race, but I happen to think you're saying, 'Well, because a Black man was elected president white voters in Arkansas revolt.' I think that's too simplistic. [I'll] tell you, Arkansas voters, as it turned out, tended to dislike Hillary Clinton more than they disliked Barack Obama."[26]

Nelson's observations are perhaps based on the fact that Obama received approximately 39 percent of the vote in Arkansas in 2008 and 37 percent four years later, while Clinton only managed just under 34 percent in 2016 and Biden approximately 35 percent in 2020.

While the term "Southern Strategy" has been used to try to explain the partisan shift among states in the former Confederacy—as Republicans made appeals to disaffected southern whites following the Civil Rights Act of 1964 and the Voting Rights Act of 1965—the explanation fails to adequately explain the decades-long shift in the South. If race alone was the factor in many southern states becoming increasingly Republican, why did it take decades to do so? And, in the case of Arkansas, why did the GOP not make significant inroads until the 2000s? Perhaps a more nuanced theory better frames the shift in southern states—including, as of late, Arkansas—to favor the GOP. Angie Maxwell and Todd Shields contend that the Southern Strategy was, in fact, a three-part, decades-long process.[27] They posit that, in addition to capturing support from disaffected whites, suspicions among conservatives regarding feminism and the political engagement of evangelical churchgoers better account for the region's political shift between the 1960s to today. However, the focus of this study is the partisan shift in Arkansas—a state that remained largely Democratic up until the end of the first decade of the twenty-first century. For Arkansas, there appeared to be little, if any, lasting political fallout for the Democratic Party brand from civil rights legislation of the 1960s. Apart from 1968, where a plurality of the state's voters supported segregationist George Wallace's third-party candidacy for president, voters in the state failed to "punish" Democrats in the decades that followed for identifying with a party that was becoming increasingly liberal with regard to social issues. The extent to which race was a factor in the success of the GOP in Arkansas during the Obama administration is an important and worthwhile consideration. However, associating the entirety of the GOP's rise and sustained success in the state (electoral success that outlived the two terms of the Obama presidency) to racism would be a gross oversimplification for the stable shift in partisanship among the electorate in the state. Nonetheless, the fact that the GOP's dramatic change in fortunes in the state begin at or around the election of Barack Obama as president cannot be ignored. Obama was not only the first African American elected to the office, but also the first non-southern Democrat to win a presidential election since John F. Kennedy in 1960. To Arkansans, particularly white conservatives in the state, the perception was that Obama was not relatable to many in ways that conflicted with or complicated their previously held personal views on race and culture in America. In an interview, Jay Barth, a political scientist and scholar of Arkansas politics, elaborated on the complicating factors of Obama, race, and cultural shifts that negatively impacted the Democratic brand in the state—particularly among white, rural Arkansans:

> Barack Obama's arrival, you know, really shifted things . . . [it] puts a new group of voters in play. You have white rural Arkansans who lived in counties that were overwhelmingly white, or at least in communities that were overwhelmingly white. There might be a county or a little hamlet here or there that was more heavily Black, but it was mostly white, white politics. And so in their daily lives, [white people] really didn't have to think about race that much. It was not part of their daily interaction. And suddenly you have this incredibly talented guy who is on their TV screens every day. And he is not only a person of color, but he is also out of sync with them in other ways . . . [this] cosmopolitan and urbane guy who did not really "get" rural America in a legitimate way. And then you throw on top his embracing of multiculturalism, including religious diversity, which was also out of sync with their experience. . . . It became a game changer in terms of how white rural Arkansans, who had been the swing voters historically . . . shift at the presidential level in 2008. Then, in 2010 the Tea Party came in and began to recruit folks, got them involved in a much more activist way [and encouraged them to run for office themselves—you started to see more and more folks run for office as Republicans. . . . [By] 2012, you see a conscious and effective campaign to link everything back to Obama: "Every vote for any Democrat is a vote for Obama." And a "vote *for* any Republican is a vote *against* Obama." And that becomes the definer. After eight years of presidency, Obama has the brand of the Democratic Party, and these rural voters—white rural voters in particular—just can't go there anymore.[28]

Governor Asa Hutchinson also discussed the effect President Obama indirectly had on the Arkansas electorate with regard to the many who had previously split their vote, but now found themselves more aligned with the GOP:

> Without any doubt, the angst about the Obama administration and Obamacare—his different policies, even [with regard to] defense, did not strike well with Arkansans. And you contrast that with the Clinton years: Clinton had a lot of scandals and an impeachment trial, but he was pragmatic and cut deals with a Republican Congress. And we actually balanced the budget during that time. I did welfare reform. There was not as big a contrast philosophically during the Clinton years as there was during the Obama years. The Obama years made Arkansans understand that they're actually conservatives, and that they did not like the direction of a progressive liberal agenda. The [government under Democratic control] outspends, is weak for America, and has government solutions [that are not] culturally conservative or pro-life. All of those distinctions made it easier for Republican candidates. And during that time the media made a difference. The rise of Fox News started earlier but gained more strength, and you had candidates running for [local offices] knocking on doors and homeowners asking, "Well, what's your position on immigration? What are you going to do about border security?" National politics [began to] impact the local elections; it was another example of the nationalization of local politics.[29]

Prior to Obama's election, Democrats in Arkansas were largely able to remind voters of their moderation and "common sense" appeals, both when Clinton was in the White House and even more so when George W. Bush—a Republican—was the most visual partisan in the country. Whether a native son was in the White House or a Republican, Arkansas Democrats had been able to expertly navigate the political landscape and operate around distinctions from their own party's national brand, utilizing candidate-centered narratives when seeking reelection. This worked for Democrats until 2010. Obama, in many ways the embodiment of a more diverse and liberal Democratic Party, simply overwhelmed the state and local politics of Arkansas. The state GOP had long been positioning and aligning themselves with their party's national brand, a consistency that has served them well in the last decade with rising conservative populism in the state and many other parts of the nation. Recalling the 2010 election cycle where Democratic incumbent Senator Blanche

Lincoln lost to Republican US House member John Boozman, Governor Hutchinson said:

> I would say the Boozman race against Blanche Lincoln probably typifies it. Because the usual strategies on the Democrat side did not work. Here you have Lincoln, who's an incumbent—and it's hard taking down incumbents. She was not only was an incumbent, but also the chair of the Senate Agriculture Committee, and everybody knows how important that is to an ag state like Arkansas. And notwithstanding all of that, they said, "That's okay. We'd rather have a Republican up there than a chairman of an ag committee." That really showed how deep the sentiment of conservative philosophy had come through our state. Before you had to persuade them that there was a difference, that you can't vote Democrat and expect conservative governance, but you didn't have to educate them anymore.[30]

Regarding the GOP branding at this time and the impact it had on Democrats in the state, the first GOP speaker of the House of Representatives in Arkansas since Reconstruction, Davy Carter, stated:

> The Republicans did a great job on branding this as "taking your healthcare away" and "socialized medicine"; they got out front of it and won that branding message. . . . It all came to a head when President Obama got elected. That's when I saw the nationalization and DC-type politics everywhere. . . . Unfairly, when President Obama got elected, and with the push for the Affordable Health Care Act [sic], that is when you started to see a complete nationalization of the state's politics. Every county judge, city council [member], school board member, [they were all] running races on "no Obamacare." It just went everywhere, and the state Democrats felt a lot of pressure, they didn't want to be identified with that. They would tell you that privately, and probably some publicly . . . that it was a drag on them. That's when, for me, all of that really came to light, and it hasn't stopped. That was the beginning of it, and it's gotten worse.[31]

Arkansas Democrats could not effectively navigate more nationalized politics in an environment where a majority of voters were not only rejecting the national Democratic politics, but also disavowing themselves of any Democratic attachment down-ticket. The GOP was poised to take advantage; the dam had broken. When asked about how the 2010 election cycle was different, as a longtime journalist covering Arkansas politics, John Brummett offered this observation:

> We had all these episodes where the Republicans would make gains, but the Democrats would block it, and come back in the next cycle. . . . But Mark Darr [was] elected lieutenant governor over Shane Broadway by a scant few votes. . . . That race was so close that it they weren't sure for a day or two exactly how it was going to go. But it was very close. So it wasn't the avalanche, it was the harbinger of the avalanche. But even so, a majority of Republicans [were] winning state constitutional offices and making gains in the legislature. They were about to take over. This is different from the spasms of inroads that the Democrats had been able to stop. It became more permanent with the Affordable Care Act and the Obama presidency, and a largely irrational revulsion in Arkansas among conservatives to [gun control] fears and those sorts of things. . . . I didn't know how stark and dramatic it would prove to be [over the next] decade.[32]

Even after the 2010 election cycle, however, there was a belief among many political elites in the state that success might not last for the GOP—a reasonable assumption at the time, given the party's unstable electoral history in the state. Brummett explained the feeling of observing this shift:

> I still thought there was a currency in Arkansas for the Mike Ross, Beebe kind of Democrat, which is a kind of Democrat that is not very Democrat on a national scale, but one connected to Arkansas and able to finesse this, "I'm an old Arkansas, south Arkansas boy, and I'm with you on the guns. And I'm with you on the cultural issues. Now, don't pay too close attention, because I want to go up here and vote for several things that Miss Pelosi would like me to vote for." I thought that could still work; I felt that later than I should have thought it. I didn't understand the change in the culture, that our politics were no longer state-based but fully nationalized, because of the internet and Fox News. I was still thinking as late as '12, maybe '14 . . . "It's not done yet. These are the two kinds of Democrats who can still win; they have a personal connection. They can have an Arkansas cultural connection, and they can finesse the liberal politics and appear more moderate." No, sir. . . . I was hit over the head with . . . the fact that people weren't buying that anymore: "Don't finesse me that you're one thing in Arkansas, something [else] in Washington. It's all national politics. It's all guns. It's all abortion. It's all taxes. It's all

health care. It's all Obama. And you're either with him or you're not." I did not fully see that coming. I thought it could still be negotiated.[33]

Independent Voters Advantage Arkansas GOP

For several decades, as previously noted, polls show that anywhere from a quarter to a third of Arkansans self-identified as independent.[34] While political changes had been afoot for some time—particularly in rural swing counties that had once been among the most staunchly Democratic, but had shown a willingness to switch to Republican candidates at the top of the ticket over the last quarter of the twentieth century—Arkansans stubbornly stuck to their party identifications, as seen in Table 3.2. Table 3.2 reports the Arkansas Poll's partisanship question between 1999 and 2021.[35] The surveys asked: "Do you think of yourself as Republican, Democrat, Independent, or other?" For this analysis, the small portion of respondents who refused or could not answer have been excluded. From 1999 to 2020, the portion of those polled who reported being an independent consistently hovers to roughly one-third of the sample while the percentage of those polled appear to decrease among Democratic identifiers and modestly increase for Republicans until more recently, when the GOP began to have a plurality of those identified.

A few observations immediately come to mind when examining the data represented in Table 3.2. First, a quick comparison between the percentage of respondents who identified as Republican in 1999 nearly doubles by 2020. Second, Democratic identifiers drop by a margin of nearly 15 percent. Third, independents remain steady throughout the period. Looking deeper, however, it is apparent that Republican identifiers only begin to consistently increase in the last decade, with a spike from the high 20 percent range to 40 percent in the final four years of data. Corresponding to the gains in Republican identifiers, the drop in Democratic identifiers increases in intensity during the last five years of the 2010s.

It is established that over the last couple decades a growing portion of Arkansans have begun to identify as Republican. Table 3.3 reports the follow-up question from the Arkansas Poll data to independents from 1999 to 2020. The table illustrates the party to which self-reported independents lean, according to the Arkansas Poll.

Self-identified independents, long a mainstay in Arkansas politics, also heavily favor the GOP. This polling data tracks well with the electoral success of the Republican Party over the last decade. Clearly, the

Table 3.2
Partisan Identification in Arkansas

Year	Republican	Democrat	Independent	Other
1999	23%	35%	31%	4%
2000	23%	36%	35%	9%
2001	27%	33%	32%	5%
2002	28%	33%	33%	3%
2003	24%	38%	31%	4%
2004	30%	35%	28%	3%
2005	23%	36%	33%	4%
2006	23%	36%	33%	3%
2007	24%	39%	30%	3%
2008	24%	35%	33%	7%
2009	24%	33%	34%	7%
2010	21%	28%	42%	7%
2011	26%	31%	34%	6%
2012	29%	31%	33%	3%
2013	24%	30%	37%	4%
2014	28%	31%	33%	3%
2015	27%	32%	32%	3%
2016	29%	25%	37%	3%
2017	29%	24%	35%	5%
2018	32%	28%	32%	6%
2019	35%	23%	31%	9%
2020	40%	21%	33%	6%

Source: The Arkansas Poll.

Table 3.3
Independents' Leaning to a Party

Year	Republican	Democrat	Independent
2000	35% (39%)	25% (26%)	35% (30%)
2001	29%	36%	31%
2002	30% (31%)	32% (34%)	33% (33%)
2003	33%	34%	33%
2004	39% (41%)	31% (32%)	30% (26%)
2005	30%	35%	32%
2006	33% (35%)	34% (34%)	30% (23%)
2007	34%	37%	29%
2008	35% (38%)	30% (29%)	33% (31%)
2009	39%	32%	27%
2010	44% (50%)	21% (16%)	33% (33%)
2011	42% (48%)	29% (28%)	26% (22%)
2012	41% (46%)	26% (22%)	28% (27%)
2013	43% (51%)	21% (22%)	31% (22%)
2014	38% (43%)	25% (23%)	30% (28%)
2015	42% (52%)	23% (20%)	30% (25%)
2016	37% (45%)	18% (19%)	40% (35%)
2017	37% (38%)	26% (26%)	32% (31%)
2018	39% (43%)	25% (25%)	35% (32%)
2019	40% (43%)	27% (31%)	31% (27%)
2020	45% (52%)	32% (30%)	19% (15%)

Source: The Arkansas Poll. Figures in parentheses indicate percentage of "likely voters."

turning point was in the period between 2008 and 2014, where Arkansas shifted from overwhelmingly Democratic to Republican with arguably no period of strong two-party competition. Table 3.3 includes the percentage of likely voters in parentheses. It is apparent that likely voters who are self-proclaimed independents favor the Republican candidates in Arkansas. Over the last decade, just under half (and in some years a majority) of these likely voters report leaning Republican.

Population Trends and Partisan Dynamics

In this chapter thus far, the focus has been entirely on the past. However, it is important to devote attention to trend data that might also help illuminate the future in the state's voting behavior, at least at the macro level. Today, as has been discussed in this chapter, Arkansas is arguably one of the most Republican-dominated states in the country. However, as the Natural State has so dramatically illustrated over the last decade, partisan politics do change. Parties change. Issues change. Voters can change—albeit slowly. While there is no crystal ball, if "demographics are destiny" as the saying goes, a glimpse into the population trends in Arkansas might give insights into the state's political future.

Today, the population of Arkansas is just over 3 million.[36] The 2020 Census showed modest growth for the state overall. Practically all of the growth was concentrated in a small number of counties in the northwestern, and—to a lesser extent—central and northeastern portions of the state. These pockets experiencing growth are the exception, not the rule, as over two-thirds of the state's seventy-five counties reportedly lost population in the preceding decade.[37] For Democrats, the population growth in Northwest Arkansas has produced a glimmer of hope to party activists organizing in the region. Not long ago, when Democrats controlled most levers of political power in Arkansas, this part of the state was the only consistently Republican-leaning region (recall that John Paul Hammerschmidt was elected to the US House of Representatives for the district encompassing this area and a Republican has held the seat ever since), but it is now home to some of the most consistent pockets of Democratic support and can claim some competitive state legislative races. This is the part of the state where one is just as likely to run into someone who had recently transplanted from another state as you would be to meet a lifetime Arkansan. Northwest Arkansas is also the most ethnically diverse part of the state with a relatively booming Hispanic population. Democrats in and around growing cities such as Fayetteville and Springdale have proven effective at contesting—and even winning—some seats in this region even as the rest of the state moves further toward the Republican column.

For much of the state, the population trend is downward. A significant portion of the state's residents live in rural areas that have consistently lost population for decades. Eastern Arkansas, with a higher proportion of African American voters—long a consistent block of support for Democratic candidates in the state—has suffered some of the most significant population losses over the last several decades. The decline in population, coupled with the changing dynamics of the state's partisan politics, was evident in the 2020 general election cycle, where Republicans managed to pick up seats in a few of the remaining rural areas with Democratic incumbent state legislators.[38] Furthermore, Republicans now enjoy significant advantages in many rural areas of Arkansas. As noted earlier, the most dramatic shift in voting behavior in the state has occurred among white rural voters—a sizeable portion of the Arkansas electorate—who now heavily advantage the GOP.[39] Even while these areas are declining in population, the decline in their relative political power is somewhat minimized by the fact that Arkansas lacks a significant metropolitan or urban population center. Instead of an urban-rural divide where significantly large population centers are densely packed and carry significant power in numbers (or votes), the divide in Arkansas is more nuanced and exists in a space that might be considered more rural-suburban or exurban—where even the areas of growth carry some characteristics of the rural areas.

Despite Northwest Arkansas offering some reasons for Democratic optimism, the foreseeable future looks particularly bright for the GOP in the state. One tool a party in power might hope to use to offset any imbalance in a region experiencing significant growth (such as Northwest Arkansas) that might prove less than predictably advantageous for that party's electoral future is redistricting. A dominant party might be able to use the reapportionment process to enhance its electoral advantage or, in the very least, plot a path that would maintain its political hold for years to come. For the first time, in 2021, state legislative and US congressional maps were drawn entirely by Republicans. More on this will be discussed in a future chapter, but this fact obviously advantages Republicans in their abilities to maintain the gains made in the previous decade and staves off most emergent Democratic advantages in the northwestern part of the state.

With this chapter, I have attempted to broadly illustrate the shift in partisanship within the Arkansas electorate and to present the perspective that partisan change in Arkansas—while seemingly occurring in a matter of one or two election cycles—was put in motion decades ago. Today, Arkansas is an overwhelmingly Republican state. Despite a smattering of Democratic pockets, the recent growth of the GOP is overwhelming, undeniable, and sustained. While the 2020 cycle highlighted how changing demographics can impact the competitiveness of statewide elections of some southern states, Arkansas does not, at the moment, appear poised to join the likes of Georgia or Texas anytime soon. The 2020 United States Census revealed only modest growth (3.3 percent) in the state and much of the overall gains in population were targeted in the northwest corner of Arkansas, while two-thirds of the state's counties recorded a loss in population over the last decade. Furthermore, the state populace remains relatively rural and largely white at a time when these factors generally favor GOP candidates. The GOP brand in Arkansas is consistent with the national party's messaging and is popular with a large enough number of Arkansans at the present time to all but guarantee statewide electoral success and an overwhelming majority of regional and local races.

Between the years 2008 and 2014, the politics of Arkansas changed in swift and dramatic fashion. In this chapter, the focus has been on the changing voting behaviors of Arkansans and the reasons for the immediate change in partisan fortunes. The absence of the Big Three in elected offices, the breakdown of the wall separating Arkansas Democrats and the national brand from which previous generations of politicians had so deftly distanced themselves, the unpopularity of President Obama, the never-ending flow of political news and entertainment, and the nationalization of partisan politics in the United States are each pieces of the puzzle that explains the seemingly sudden switch in partisan loyalties in the state. However, for lasting change to occur, and for the gains the GOP made in these few election cycles to hold (or expand even further), events and changes had to take place long before to bring about what we see today in Arkansas—an established political dominance by a party that, as recently as 2010, saw its gubernatorial candidate lose every county in the state. The following chapters will shift from what V. O. Key once considered the party in the electorate to the two major party organizations and, finally, the party in government.

4

STATE PARTY ORGANIZATIONS AND THE RISE OF THE GOP IN ARKANSAS

Often overlooked, state party organizations can be a powerful source for candidate recruitment, fundraising, data aggregation, and voter mobilization. From 2005 to 2015, Arkansas's political environment underwent unprecedented change. A part of the once "Solid South," Arkansas—by 2015—was represented by Republicans in all six federal offices. Additionally, for the first time since Reconstruction, Republicans enjoyed majorities in both state legislative chambers and could boast just the fourth Republican governor in nearly 150 years. This chapter considers the state's partisan change in the lens of V. O. Key Jr.'s tripartite of political party with an assessment of the changes that occurred to the state's two major party organizations over this time.[1] In this chapter, survey data from a 1999 study is compared to a 2013 examination of state party organizations to evaluate the changes that have taken place with regard to the operations and organizational strength of both state parties in a time of political change in the Natural State. The analysis of this data reveals that changes undergone over this period by each state party organization resulted in stronger, more capable state political parties, overall. However, the data also indicates the state's Republican Party made the most substantive gains in terms of organization and professionalization.

Portions of the material presented in this chapter were previously published in the *Midsouth Political Science Review* (15, no. 2 [2014]: 81–102) and are reprinted here with permission.

The Republican Party of Arkansas was developing a statewide organizational giant over the last two decades and this organizational strengthening is one of the reasons for the party's historical gains in the state over the last decade.

In 1999, John Aldrich, Brad Gomez, and John Griffin conducted the "State Party Organizations Study." This survey assessed the role of state party organizations in an increasingly candidate-centered environment.[2] More recently, in 2013, Drew Kurlowski and I sought to update and build upon this previous work to evaluate the changes that have taken place with regard to the operations and organizational strength of state parties.[3] By comparing the results of these two surveys, the following analyzes the Arkansas Democratic and Republican state party organizations over a period of significant change, from 1999 to 2013—aligning conveniently with this book's time frame.

For most of the time that Democrats dominated electoral politics in the state, the Democratic Party of Arkansas—as a statewide party organization—did not exist in any meaningful way. As Key, Blair, and others pointed out, the Democratic Party was primarily composed of several loose and fluid groups, or coalitions, organized (in the loosest sense of the word) around an individual and based primarily on personality, personal loyalties, perceived slights, et cetera.[4] The Democratic Party's long-held grip on state politics was not characterized by the kind of centralized control one might ascribe to a party machine, nor did the party boast an organizational structure that operated in coordination with county-level organizations to recruit candidates and fundraise—as is the case today. As much as the Democrats lacked organizational structure, the Republican Party—with the exception of a few areas in the northwest corner of the state—was virtually nonexistent. According to Diane Blair, who reflected on the two parties leading up to the Rockefeller era of the 1960s: "Arkansas had essentially a no-party system, with two very elitist and ephemeral organizations that called themselves parties but that rarely met, had no significant electoral purposes, and no discernible value to the voters (except that the Democrats did manage staff, and pay for the primary elections)."[5]

It would take the personal funds and zealous will of Winthrop Rockefeller to build a modern Republican Party of Arkansas in the late 1960s and a Democratic scare following the reelection loss of Governor Bill Clinton, who lost unexpectedly to Republican Frank White in 1980, to see any discernable signs of two, albeit still weak, state party organizations in Arkansas. Throughout much of the second half of the twentieth century, despite momentary enhancements of the state party organizations, both parties struggled financially and lagged behind their respective co-partisans in other states in terms of staffing, fundraising, recruitment, and messaging operations. However, there was evidence of GOP organizational strength in the 1990s. Following the hotly contested Republican nomination for governor in 1990, the Republican Party of Arkansas elected Asa Hutchinson and Sheffield Nelson as cochairmen of the state organization. Hutchinson had been the Republican nominee for attorney general in 1990 but lost to Winston Bryant. Nelson had won the 1990 primary over Tommy Robinson, only to lose to incumbent governor Clinton in the general election. Hutchinson and Nelson would work together to unify the party until 1993, when Nelson took on a leadership role within the national GOP and Hutchinson retained his role as chair until 1995—at which point, he left to seek a seat in the US House of Representatives. In his history of the Republican Party of Arkansas, Ken Coon credits Hutchinson and Nelson with successfully unifying the party after a bruising GOP primary for governor that saw more interest among Arkansas voters than any other GOP contest.[6]

Despite the GOP in Arkansas certainly enhancing its organizational presence in the state in the 1990s, much ground was yet to be gained in terms of objective measures of party strength—a historical characteristic of both the Republican and Democratic parties of Arkansas. While historical context is important in explaining the weak party organizations in the state in the second half of the twentieth century—which also aligns with the first generation of the modern GOP in Arkansas—the focus of this chapter is the transition from Democratic to Republican dominance in the state at the turn of the twenty-first century to the early 2020s. In doing so, I assess the progression of each party organization in such a way that allows for comparisons from the years when Democrats were still safely dominant in the state's politics to a more recent time when the GOP began to make historical gains in winning elections. In addition to evaluating the changes these two state party organizations have undergone since the late twentieth century to today, this chapter also addresses the organizational strength of these parties with a particular focus into their institutional characteristics, degree of coordination with their respective national committees, roles in campaign issue development, candidate recruitment, and candidate support. In order to assess the changes undergone in these two state party organizations, the survey results of each are reported and the findings of Aldrich et al.'s study are compared with those of Davis and Kurlowski's. Additionally, David Dulio and R. Sam Garrett's party organization strength index is used to assess the extent to which changes among these two-party organizations have occurred since the late 1990s.[7]

In 1999, Aldrich, Gomez, and Griffin facilitated a survey-based study of state party organizations. Reaching out to all one hundred major state party organizations, the study boasted a 64 percent response rate. Survey questionnaires were mailed specifically to state party chairs. Aldrich and his colleagues' effort was a useful update to Cotter, Gibson, Bibby, and Huckshorn's work and accounted for the condition of state party organizations leading up to the twenty-first century.[8] Unlike the data collected by Cotter and his colleagues, this survey's state-identifiable results are publicly available.[9] The 1999 study reported data that had been collected over the course of several years.

In 2013, Davis and Kurlowski began distributing an updated state organizational survey in order to assess changes that had taken place over the nearly fifteen years since the effort by Aldrich et al. Unlike the earlier study, the questions for this survey were not directed to any one staff member of a state party's organization, enabling state chairpersons, executive directors, or anyone else knowledgeable and authorized to participate in the survey.[10] While some of the surveys were conducted over the phone, the majority of responses were completed online using Qualtrics®. It is important to note that despite the differences in survey delivery systems, the question wording was identical. The Republican Party of Arkansas's survey was conducted over the phone while the Arkansas Democratic Party's was completed online. As was agreed before the administering of each survey, the names and positions of the individuals who participated remain anonymous.

The respondent for the Democratic Party of Arkansas reported that the organization's chairperson served at a full-time capacity but did not receive a salary. Earlier, in the Aldrich et al. study, the position was reported to have been a part-time position. In 2013, the chair position remained term-limited. Regarding office staff, the party maintained a public relations director and a full-time executive director. As of 2013, the Democratic Party of Arkansas reported employing a field staff, conducting direct mail fundraising, operating "get out the vote" (GOTV) programs, and conducting public opinion surveys. In terms of party contributions to different campaigns for state and congressional office, the party reported giving to all levels except local positions—consistent with the party's reported contribution behavior in 1999.

Another aspect of the survey that addresses the institutional characteristics of the state party office is the staff and budget differential between election years and nonelection years. During election years, the Democratic Party of Arkansas reported in 2013 an estimated budget of $3.5 million and a staff of seventy-three employees (seventy full-time, three part-time). In a year when no regular elections are held, the party cuts back significantly with a budget estimation of $750,000 and a staff of six. The scaling down during nonelection years is consistent with the average calculated from all respondents for the 2013 survey.

The Democratic Party of Arkansas reported one of the highest numbers of election-year staff of any participating state party organization in the Davis and Kurlowski survey. The discrepancy in election-year funding and staffing to that of nonelection years offers insight into the priorities and purpose of the organization and is worth closer investigation. The dramatic increase in reported election-year staff is—in part—explained by the party's use of a coordinated campaign. The Democratic Party's respondent offered the following regarding the coordinated campaign: "The Party operates a coordinated campaign in election year [sic] which campaigns buy into [sic] but it's normally not included in the campaign budget. They raise money for the coordinated campaign and then gain the benefits of a strong coordinated campaign."[11]

This coordinated effort between the party organization and its candidates explains the high number of election-year staff reported in the 2013 survey (seventy-three total)—as these individuals serve to assist those Democratic candidates who invest in the coordinated campaign. In addition, the fact that candidates reportedly "buy into" the coordinated campaign suggests their own investments into the program provide a portion of support required for such an increase in election-year staff.

Table 4.1 provides a comparison of the party's institutional characteristics between the findings of the 2013 Davis and Kurlowski survey and the 1999 Aldrich et al. study. In the earlier survey, the party reported that it did not employ research staff or a public relations director. Apart from the growth in staff over the last several years, the organization's budget has also increased—a prerequisite for the dramatic increase in the number of overall election-year staff. While a modest increase in the nonelection-year budget is reported between the two studies (just short of $700,000 in 1999—adjusting for inflation—to $750,000 in 2013), the party's election-year budget dramatically increased from nearly $2.1 million (adjusted for inflation) reported in 1999 to $3.5 million in 2013. The

Table 4.1
Democratic Party of Arkansas Institutional Characteristics

Institutional Characteristics	Davis and Kurlowski, 2013	Aldrich, Gomez, and Griffin, 1999
Chair position, full-time	Yes	No
Chair position, term-limited	Yes	—
State party chair, salaried	No	No
Annual salary	—	—
Contributed to governor	Yes	Yes
Contributed to other constitutional offices	Yes	Yes
Contributed to congressional offices	Yes	Yes
Contributed to state senator	Yes	Yes
Contribute to state legislator	Yes	Yes
Contributed to county or local offices	No	No
Held fundraising event	Yes	Yes
Direct mail fundraising program	Yes	Yes
Employed research staff	Yes	No
Employed public relations director	Yes	No
Employed full-time executive director	Yes	Yes
Employed field staff	Yes	Yes
Employed comptroller/bookkeeper	Yes	Yes
Conducted campaign seminars	Yes	Yes
Recruited full slate of candidates	Yes	Yes
Published a newspaper/newsletter/magazine	Yes	Yes
Operated voter registration programs	Yes	No
Conducted public opinion surveys	Yes	Yes
Typical election-year budget	$3.5 million	$2,097,452[12]
Typical election-year full-time staff	70	8
Typical election-year part-time staff	3	4
Typical nonelection-year budget	$750K	$699,151[13]
Typical nonelection-year full-time staff	5	4
Typical nonelection-year part-time staff	1	0

party now reports employing research staff and a public relations director, increasing its level of organizational sophistication. Additionally, the increased budget and staff during election years suggest strong electioneering efforts on behalf of the state party organization.

A representative for the Republican Party of Arkansas also provided information regarding the party's institutional characteristics, allowing for a comparison of the party today to the organization at the time of the Aldrich et al. study.

The chair of the Republican Party of Arkansas is a paid, full-time position. Unlike the Democratic Party's chair, who does not receive a salary, the Republican state organization reported paying the chairperson between $50,000 and $75,000 annually in 2013. This is a change from what the organization reported in 1999. At the time of the Aldrich et al. study, the survey participant selected the answer option reading, "State party considered job part-time but it is actually full time." At that time, the Republican Party chairperson did not receive a salary.

In 2013, the Republican Party of Arkansas reported that it contributed to all levels of state office and US Congress, but does not contribute to local races—a change from the organization's reported actions in 1999. The extent of involvement in contributing to different levels of office is of interest particularly given the changing nature of campaign contributions in American politics over the last several decades. Between the end of the "soft money" era and the proliferation of advocacy group spending, one might expect state party organization involvement in financial contributions to have changed since the 1990s.

Much like the Democrats, the Republican Party had hired additional specialized staff since the earlier survey. In 2013, the party reported having a public relations director. A comparison of the party's reported election-year budget to its nonelection-year budget is not possible, as the nonelection-year amount was not reported. The reported nonelection-year budget in 1999 was $500,000 or—accounting for inflation—$699,151 at the time of the 2013 survey. Accounting for inflation, the reported election-year budget appears to have increased only modestly from $2,097,452 in 1999 to approximately $2.2 million in 2013. The numbers of overall election-year and nonelection-year staff did not change over this time period. Unlike the Democratic Party, the Republican Party did not report a change in the overall number of staff from election to nonelection years. Table 4.2 provides a comparison of the Republican Party's institutional characteristics between the findings of the 2013 and 1999 studies.

Table 4.2
Republican Party of Arkansas Institutional Characteristics

Institutional Characteristics	Davis and Kurlowski, 2013	Aldrich, Gomez, and Griffin, 1999
Chair position, full-time	Yes	No
Chair position, term-limited	Yes	—
State party chair, salaried	Yes	No
Annual salary	$50K–75K	—
Contributed to governor	Yes	Yes
Contributed to other constitutional offices	Yes	Yes
Contributed to congressional offices	Yes	Yes
Contributed to state senator	Yes	Yes
Contribute to state legislator	Yes	Yes
Contributed to county or local offices	No	Yes
Held fundraising event	Yes	Yes
Direct mail fundraising program	Yes	Yes
Employed research staff	No	Yes
Employed public relations director	Yes	No
Employed full-time executive director	Yes	Yes
Employed field staff	Yes	Yes
Employed comptroller/bookkeeper	No	Yes
Conducted campaign seminars	Yes	Yes
Recruited full slate of candidates	Yes	Yes
Published a newspaper/newsletter/magazine	Yes	Yes
Operated voter registration programs	Yes	No
Conducted public opinion surveys	Yes	Yes
Typical election-year budget	$2.2 million	$2,097,452[14]
Typical election-year full-time staff	8	5
Typical election-year part-time staff	0	3
Typical nonelection-year budget	—	$699,151[15]
Typical nonelection-year full-time staff	4	3
Typical nonelection-year part-time staff	0	1

Both party organizations have changed somewhat with regard to institutional characteristics since the late 1990s. The Democratic Party of Arkansas reports a significantly larger election-year budget and election-year staff between the two surveys. The dramatic increases in election-year budget and staff are likely explained by the party's unique coordinated campaign effort whereby candidates reportedly "buy into" the effort in order to benefit from the sources of the party organization. While the survey data provides little insight into the direct relationship of budgetary capability and staffing, the increase in election-year staff reported by the Democratic Party strongly suggests a large portion of the organization's increased budget has funded the coordinated campaign effort. The Republican Party of Arkansas reports only slight changes in the number of staff and even less in regard to budget, but boasts a full-time, salaried chair and other traits of increased institutional sophistication including the addition of a public relations director. Overall, a comparison of institutional characteristics suggests each state organization is stronger today than they were at the end of the twentieth century. The organization that has undergone the most change in regard to these measures is the Democratic Party of Arkansas.

Candidate Recruitment

Given that parties seek to gain control of government by winning elections, recruiting candidates for office is a natural role of any state party organization. While the literature on the topic continues to enhance our knowledge of alternative origins of candidate recruitment—such as citizen groups, political elites, and state legislative leaders—previous studies surveying those within party organizations report active involvement in recruiting.[16] However, the issue might suffer from response bias, as studies asking candidates to report the nature and extent to which state parties actively recruit individuals have called parties' involvement into question. Thomas Kazee and Mary Thornberry raise doubts that state parties play particularly active roles in recruiting candidates for Congress, specifically.[17] Additional evidence of limited state party recruitment for seats in the US House is found in Kazee's edited volume.[18] Thus, it is possible that state party organizations overstate their involvement in recruiting efforts. With this caveat, the results from both state party organizations in the 2013 survey concerning candidate recruitment are compared to the reported levels of involvement from the 1999 study. Each survey respondent was prompted with the following question,

"Please describe the level of involvement of the state party in recruiting candidates for the following offices as Active, Limited, or Not Involved."

In 1999, the Democratic Party of Arkansas reported active involvement in recruiting at all levels of government except for local and county offices. In 2013, the party's survey participant reported limited party involvement in recruiting for governor and US Senate, and active recruitment efforts for local and county offices. Why the change? It appears the party focused its attention on recruiting for offices highest on the ballot in 1999 but has since shifted the organization's attention more toward recruiting and cultivating political talent at the local level. Term limits—enacted in the state in 1992—began to impact the Arkansas House and Senate in 1998 and 2000, respectively, and have likely directed more attention to recruiting state legislators over the last fifteen years.[19]

Table 4.3
Democratic Party of Arkansas Involvement in Candidate Recruitment

Candidate Recruitment	Davis and Kurlowski, 2013	Aldrich, Gomez, and Griffin, 1999
Governor	Limited	Active
Other state Constitutional offices	Active	Active
US House	Active	Active
US Senate	Limited	Active
State legislator	Active	Active
Local and county offices	Active	Limited

While the survey results from the state Democratic organization suggest a shift in recruiting efforts, the Republican Party of Arkansas claimed the same levels of involvement in candidate recruitment in 2013 as the earlier Aldrich et al. study. They reported active involvement at the gubernatorial level, other state Constitutional offices, as well as all legislative levels, and reported limited involvement at the local and county level.

Table 4.4
Republican Party of Arkansas Involvement in Candidate Recruitment

Candidate Recruitment	Davis and Kurlowski, 2013	Aldrich, Gomez, and Griffin, 1999
Governor	Active	Active
Other state Constitutional offices	Active	Active
US House	Active	Active
US Senate	Active	Active
State legislator	Active	Active
Local and county offices	Limited	Limited

Campaign Issue Development

One question asked by Aldrich and his colleagues was, "During your tenure as state party chair, has the state party organization developed campaign issues or has this normally been left to the candidates?" This question was asked again by Davis and Kurlowski without specifically addressing the respective state party organization's chair. In both surveys, the Democratic Party of Arkansas reported to jointly develop campaigns issues with candidates. The Republican state party organization reportedly left the development of campaign issues to their candidates in 1999 but reported being jointly involved in the process in 2013.

Candidate Support

In addition to institutional characteristics, previous literature suggests the level of support a party organization provides its candidates is a function of its organizational structure.[20] Aldrich et al. asked party chairpersons to report whether they performed several electioneering and party building activities with county party organizations. However, Davis and Kurlowski sought to learn the extent of the coordination between the state organization and its candidates. Therefore, the 2013 survey question regarding candidate support read: "Has the state party organization participated in any of the following activities with candidates?" The difference in word usage from "county party organizations" to "candidates" could have potentially produced different survey responses.

The results are presented for comparison in Table 4.5. Overall, both party organizations indicated providing more candidate support in 2013 than they did in 1999. The Democratic Party of Arkansas reported coordinating joint fundraising, GOTV efforts, and voter registration drives with its candidates.[21] The Arkansas Republican Party reportedly carried out all four types of candidate support—as indicated in the 2013 survey.

Table 4.5
Comparison of Reported Candidate / County Committee Support Activities

Candidate Support	Davis and Kurlowski, 2013 Democratic Party of Arkansas	Davis and Kurlowski, 2013 Republican Party of Arkansas	Aldrich, Gomez, and Griffin, 1999 Democratic Party of Arkansas	Aldrich, Gomez, and Griffin, 1999 Republican Party of Arkansas
Shared mailing lists	No	Yes	Yes*	Yes*
Joint fundraising	Yes	Yes	No*	No*
Participated in GOTV	Yes	Yes	Yes*	Yes*
Voter registration drives	Yes	Yes	No*	No*

Note: * indicates Aldrich et al. survey response to question regarding support offered to county committees.

Coordination with National Committee

Cotter and Bibby, Jackson and Hitlin, and Huckshorn et al. reported increased collaboration between the two national parties and their respective state organizations.[22] Cotter et al. provided convincing cross-sectional evidence of state-national party integration.[23] However, the topic is complicated by interparty differences between Democratic and Republican committees. William Crotty asserts that—with regard to party rules concerning delegate selection—Democratic Party reforms in the 1970s empowered the Democratic National Committee while diminishing the autonomy of the party's state organizations.[24] However, Charles Longley warns against overstating the party centralization thesis.[25] Citing disputes related to national convention delegate selection, Gary Wekkin proposes these changes in the Democratic Party power structure created a "two-way street" conceptualized within Wright's framework of intergovernmental relations.[26] Regarding the Republican Party, Bibby observed: "Unlike the Democratic National Committee, which has asserted control over the presidential nominating process, the RNC has achieved increased power and an enlarged role in the political system by performing or supplementing the campaign functions previously thought to be the exclusive domain of state party or candidate organizations."[27]

Aldrich and his colleagues asked the state chairpersons how often they dealt with their respective national committees on the following issues: federal appointments, speakers, assisting state candidates, fundraising, national convention activities, and implementing national committee programs. This same question was asked more broadly by Davis and Kurlowski in 2013, and Table 4.6 and Table 4.7 report these surveys' results regarding this line of questioning for both the Democratic Party and Republican Party of the state, respectively. While both surveys neglect the issue of organizational interactions concerning presidential nominations specifically, much can be assessed from the data available.

The Democratic Party of Arkansas—in both surveys—reported regular coordination with the Democratic National Committee (DNC). The results of the 2013 survey suggested the existence of a lasting, integrated partnership between the two organizations. With exception to federal appointments and patronage and the implementation of national committee programs, the state party reported to regularly coordinate with the DNC.

Table 4.6

Democratic Party of Arkansas's Coordination with the Democratic National Committee

Coordination with DNC	Davis and Kurlowski, 2013	Aldrich, Gomez, and Griffin, 1999
Federal appointments	Never	Occasionally
Speakers	Regularly	Regularly
Assisting state candidates	Regularly	Occasionally
Fundraising	Regularly	Regularly
National convention	Regularly	Regularly
Implementing national committee programs	Occasionally	Regularly

The earlier Aldrich et al. data reported the Republican Party of Arkansas never coordinated with the Republican National Committee (RNC) regarding federal appointments. While the party reportedly reached out to the RNC regularly to gain assistance for state candidates and general fundraising, the state party only occasionally worked with the organization to obtain political speakers, assist in the implementation of RNC programs, and coordinate national convention activities.

Overall, the state party's responses to the same questions posed in 2013 suggested increased levels of coordination. In 2013, the Republican Party of Arkansas reported to occasionally coordinate with the RNC concerning federal appointments, patronage, and fundraising. Additionally, the state organization reported to regularly work with the RNC to obtain speakers (at the time of the interview, the survey respondent volunteered that the state party was hosting Senator Rand Paul of Kentucky), assist state candidates, implement RNC programs, and participate in national convention activities. In short, a comparison of these two surveys suggests an increased interdependence between the RNC and the state party organization—circumstantial evidence in support of Bibby's earlier conclusion.[28]

Table 4.7

Republican Party of Arkansas's Coordination with the Republican National Committee

Coordination with RNC	Davis and Kurlowski, 2013	Aldrich, Gomez, and Griffin, 1999
Federal appointments	Occasionally	Never
Speakers	Regularly	Occasionally
Assisting state candidates	Regularly	Regularly
Fundraising	Occasionally	Regularly
National convention	Regularly	Occasionally
Implementing national committee programs	Regularly	Occasionally

Party Organizational Strength

Existing literature on party organizations assesses strength based largely on the institution's characteristics and ability to provide resources to their candidates. It is believed that stronger state party organizations possess the institutional capacities to attain their electoral ends. Using the Aldrich et al. survey data, Dulio and Garrett created an index of state party organizational strength. In their study, responses from what I have categorized as *institutional characteristics, candidate recruitment*, and *candidate support* were each given a value of 0 or 1, where the combined minimum score of overall organizational strength was 0 out of 15 and a maximum score was 15 out of 15. Based on the Aldrich et al. survey data, the Democratic Party of Arkansas scored a 9 out of 15 and the Republican Party of Arkansas scored a 10 out of 15 when surveyed in 1999.

Using the 2013 survey data and assessing the two state party organizations on the same criteria as Dulio and Garrett, the Democratic Party of Arkansas scores 13 out of 15 and the Republican Party of Arkansas scores 15 out of 15.[29] A simple quantification, Dulio and Garrett's index allows me to compare the organizational strength of these two parties at two points in time. The results provide further evidence that both state parties are stronger organizations in 2013 they were at the close of the twentieth century, but the GOP had made greater strides in their development and capabilities.

Much can be gleaned by comparing the data from these two state party organization surveys. A great deal has changed in Arkansas's political landscape since the Aldrich et al. study. The Republican Party of Arkansas has enjoyed unprecedented success in the state over the last several elections. As recently as 2008, the party had difficulty convincing viable candidates to challenge incumbent congressional Democrats. By 2013—at the time the state party data was collected—five of the state's six congressional seats are held by Republicans. The GOP has also enjoyed unprecedented success at the state legislative level. The goal of this chapter has been to assess the dramatic partisan shift in the state through the lens of party organization and address what, if any, changes occurred that might, in part, explain the GOP gains in the state.

The survey analysis presented leads me to conclude that the Democratic Party of Arkansas and the Republican Party of Arkansas both grew stronger between 1999 and 2013 in terms of staffing, budget size (to varying degrees), and organizational sophistication. The Democratic Party's reported increase in election-year budget and overall election-year staff is the most noteworthy change between the Aldrich et al. and Davis and Kurlowski surveys. The increase appears to be explained by the organization's utilization of a coordinated campaign effort whereby candidates collaborate in order to collectively benefit from the resources of the party. Also, both parties appear to have increased their means of candidate support. While some may see the Democratic Party of Arkansas's self-reported decrease in candidate recruitment at the gubernatorial and US Senate levels as evidence of lost influence in the political processes of state politics, I believe it is more likely the case that term limits—which were applied to state legislators in the late 1990s—prompted more focus on recruitment for these impacted positions. Despite term limits taking effect, the Republican state organization reported being actively involved in all levels of candidate recruitment apart from local and county offices. Of course, as previously stated, findings regarding party organization involvement in recruiting need to be presented with caution, as previous studies on candidate recruitment suggest the possibility of response bias.

How much stock are we to take from the reported state party organizational enhancements made by both parties between 1999 and 2013? Can the electoral gains by Republicans, resulting in a transition period from Democratic dominance to increased two-party competition to near-total Republican rule, be—at least in part—explained by the increased party organizational strength? Given the electoral gains seen between the years of both studies, it appears the Arkansas Republican Party's state organization had gained in its ability to assist its candidates for office over the years. It is perhaps more difficult to reconcile the idea that the Democratic Party of Arkansas had also improved in terms of organizational strength over the same time period while suffering electoral losses of historical proportions during the latter years of the analysis. However, this too can be explained. Dwaine Marvick once wrote, "In any electoral democracy, there are reasons why rival party organizations in the same locality will look somewhat alike. There are functional grounds for expecting considerable performance symmetry."[30] The state GOP made considerable gains between the years 1999 and 2013 that helped position itself ready to assist the party's goal in winning elections. Meanwhile, the Democratic state operation also enhanced its capabilities. Since the Aldrich et al. survey, the Democratic Party not only increased its election-year budget, but dramatically retooled its electioneering efforts that resulted in a significantly larger number of election-year staff via the coordinated campaign. The findings reported here provide an additional case in support for previous studies that have reported a positive relationship between state two-party electoral competition and organizational sophistication.[31] However, the GOP has since enjoyed historical success and Democrats now find themselves in much the same condition Republicans did decades ago—the minority party in a one-party-dominated state. What does this mean? Party organizational strength is just one piece of a multivariate puzzle in explaining the ascendance of the GOP in the Natural State. The Republican Party of Arkansas, particularly under the leadership of Chairman Doyle Webb, found itself poised to capitalize on the Republicans' gaining control of the state's partisan politics. The party organization undoubtedly played a significant role in the increase in Republican control between 2005 and 2015 (and the dominance of the party that continues to the present day), but it is just one of many contributing elements that led to the rise of the GOP in the state. Based on the evidence of this chapter, it can be reported that the Republican Party of Arkansas had increased its organizational capabilities prior to the post-2010 election cycles—which strongly suggests the organization played a key role in the success of the party moving forward. However, success breeds success. In the years since the Davis and Kurlowski data was collected, the GOP in Arkansas has reached such heights in all facets of the state's politics that the Natural State is no more competitive two-party state today than it was decades ago when Democrats enjoyed a similar dominance.

It appears that, at least for a time, the Republican Party's state-level electoral gains increased interparty competition in Arkansas. This observation is supported by previous research on the topic. Austin Ranney wrote that southern states in the mid-twentieth century possessed moderate to weak party systems.[32] This lack of party strength in the region was attributed to long-term Democratic Party domination in southern states. Key wrote that the region was almost entirely Democratic and, despite strong intraparty factions, southern states were dominated by Democratic politics. This one-party domination led to an unorganized Democratic Party and nonexistent Republican Party structures until the 1960s.[33] Over the last three decades, several southern states have experienced increased two-party competition. Morehouse and Jewell contend this increase has resulted in more disciplined and capable parties.[34] The reported changes undergone by Arkansas's Democratic and Republican state party organizations, over the years captured in this analysis, provide circumstantial evidence supporting previous studies on this relationship—particularly among other southern states. To date, the data for the Davis and Kurlowski analysis was conducted several years and a few elections cycles ago. Since then the Democratic Party of Arkansas has suffered from financial instability and recruitment struggles, while the Republican Party in Arkansas has flourished to previously unknown heights.[35]

Doyle Webb expanded on the importance of organization in contributing to the success of the Republican Party of Arkansas:

> Clearly, the first responsibility of the state party is to establish the brand of the party. What do I mean by that? What does it mean to be a Republican in Arkansas? What do we stand for? What can you, the voter, identify with? I think our first responsibility is establishing that brand. The second purpose for a state party, particularly in Arkansas, was to establish affiliate organizations. In every county we call them "county committees." So that you have an organization in [each] county. From my perspective [the Democrats] didn't have to organize at the local level, because [their] organization was the courthouse and the elected officials at the courthouse; we had none of that. So establishing those county committees [was crucial], finding individuals that were identified with the brand and supportive of the brand, and then helping to target, recruit, and support candidates at every level. County committees would be responsible at the county level, but fledgling county committees can't always do what needs to be done. The state party needs to [serve as] a model. . . . I think the brand is the key. And sometimes the brand is defined by the gubernatorial candidate or the top of the ticket . . . but you have to continue to talk about the brand and not confuse [it].[36]

Contextualizing this analysis, the GOP in Arkansas underwent significant change in regard to its leadership late in the time period when the data were collected. In 2009, Webb, former state senator and chief of staff to Lieutenant Governor Winthrop Paul Rockefeller, was elected chair of the Arkansas Republican Party. It was at this point when the party decided to pay the chair of the state organization a salary—ensuring a full-time commitment to the duties of the office. At that time, according to Webb, the party was struggling.[37] However, through the next decade, the state organization sought to grow its presence at the county level and enhance the party's brand around the state. Coinciding with the rise of the Tea Party movement, and a majority of Arkansans disapproving of the job performance of President Barack Obama, the state GOP was poised to capitalize on the political opportunities presented by couching the Democratic Party as out of step with Arkansas values—a messaging struggle long-fought by more moderate Democrats in Arkansas that, at this point, would become an unsurmountable obstacle.

The state party organization cannot solely be held responsible for the gains or losses of a party. Generally, the functions of the state parties are to fundraise, recruit, campaign for, and generally support the partisans and promote the brand of the respective party. While it may very well be the case that strong party organizations are often correlated with an intrastate competitive two-party system, the past (and not so past) history of Arkansas politics is largely placed within times when one party dominates the state's partisan politics. For most of its political history, Arkansas has been a one-party state dominated by Democrats. More recent events suggest the state is now once again controlled by one party, the Republican Party. The time period between 1999 and 2013 may very well have captured the only time in the state's history where we have seen two truly competitive parties in Arkansas and that is likely the explanation for each organization's reporting an increase in organizational strength during that time. In short, two-party organization leads to stronger party organizations, but the inverse may not be true. What cannot yet be captured at the publishing of this book are the long-term effects of Democratic Party decline and Republican Party dominance on the respective state party organization in Arkansas.

It is possible to overstate the significance of a state party organization —especially in Arkansas. Democrats enjoyed over a century of dominance despite lacking any strong formal statewide organization and the electoral gains made by the Republican Party more recently cannot be solely attributed to the enhanced organizational structure within the state. However, while the changes between the period studied here indicate stronger organization for both parties, significant strides within the GOP organization coincided with other political factors that allowed the party to capitalize on opportunities for growth and unprecedented electoral success. As a measure, and one indicator of the party's recent success, the GOP state party organization has significantly enhanced its functionality. As the political winds changed in Arkansas, the state's Republican Party organization was poised to seize the opportunity.

5

STATE GOVERNMENT AND THE RISE OF THE GOP IN ARKANSAS

In this chapter, I aim to contextualize the impact of this dramatic partisan shift in the state and the challenges of one-party rule—something Arkansans had experienced for decades prior to the current political environment.

Previous research on the state's governmental institutions largely covered the time frame I identify as the first and second generation of the modern Republican Party in the state. These studies include Diane Blair's *Arkansas Politics and Government: Do the People Rule?*, Richard Wang and Michael Dougan's edited volume *Arkansas Politics: A Reader*, and Walter Nunn's *Readings in Arkansas Government*, to name a few. Studies on Arkansas government prior to the mid-twentieth century depict a largely incompetent and corrupt collection of political institutions and actors failing their fledgling state and its residents. Regarding the politics and state government in post–World War II Arkansas, V. O. Key Jr. observed:

> A number of Arkansawyers that have more than passing acquaintance with other states and hence standards by which to judge, regard plain, simple, clean government as their state's most pressing need. It is indicative of the content of the state's politics that they feel this battle must be

fought out before any item of real importance can be put on the political agenda. They conceive Arkansas's first problem to be the establishment of the essential mechanisms of democratic government. Since World War II it has been precisely that problem that has generated principal controversy in the state. It would seem that in Arkansas, more than in almost any other southern state, social and economic issues of significance to the people have lain ignored in the confusion and paralysis of disorganized factional politics.

He goes on to note that these factions were not based on articulated ideological lines:

> In Arkansas, former governors, unsuccessful gubernatorial candidates, and newspaper reporters deny the existence of even the vaguest sort of grouping of voters and political leaders along conservative-progressive lines. This does not mean that there are no politicians of liberal leanings ... or of conservative inclinations ... or that occasions do not occur when individuals of like policy-disposition act in concert. But, much as in Florida, there have not developed in Arkansas alignments of political leaders organized to give effective expression to differences in political viewpoint. Nor have there developed continuing groupings of voters along liberal-conservative lines.[1]

Instead of policy debates, conflicts arose along personal or regional lines that often led to more neglect of the populace. However, as many other states began to professionalize and modernize their state institutions—particularly, state legislatures—Arkansas appeared to follow suit.[2] The election of Winthrop Rockefeller was driven largely by a diverse collection of reform-minded progressives and others tired of the politics of the Faubus era.

Rockefeller's election—as the first Republican governor since Reconstruction—was a dramatic shift in the state's history. However, for the well-established Democratic majorities in both chambers of the Arkansas General Assembly, Rockefeller's presence in the governor's mansion appeared a mere speed bump—rather than a roadblock—to the Democrat-dominated House and Senate. As stated earlier in this book, Rockefeller's two terms in office, while an inspired and hopeful call for reform by voters, resulted in limited substantive change in the operation of the state's government, as some of Rockefeller's initiatives failed outright or—in the case of state government reorganization efforts—were held up until after his leaving office by the Democratic legislature. Thus, Arkansas government continued to be a one-party-dominated state to the extent that the state's political dynamics hardly resembled party-oriented politics at all.

This chapter's primary focus is to explore the challenges and impact of historic partisan change in the state's government in the years following 2010—the third generation of the modern GOP in Arkansas. Interviews from observers as well as officeholders offer firsthand accounts of the obstacles and substantive changes to state government that occurred since the partisan shift in Arkansas. Throughout the chapter, I ask the reader to consider the risks of one-party dominance—a theme consistently woven into the political fabric of Arkansas. Now, it appears the state has decisively traded one-party rule at the hands of Democrats for one-party rule at the hands of Republicans. However, the intraparty conflict—a natural occurrence when virtually all statewide partisan contests are settled in the dominant party's primaries—is taking place in a very different political era than before. This new environment in Arkansas— one influenced more by national political issues and branding in a more polarizing political space—results in a stronger focus on ideological purity and distinctly more conservative policy than in the recent past.

By the Numbers: The GOP in Arkansas Government

The partisan shift in the state, beginning in 2010 and becoming more pronounced over time, is perhaps most simply illustrated by examining the partisan balance in the Arkansas General Assembly. Table 5.1 reports the partisan makeup of the House in the Arkansas General Assembly from 1992 to 2020. As recently as 2008—a pivotal time in the state's politics—Democrats gained seats. However, in 2010, Republicans picked up a significant number of seats and, since then, have expanded their advantage in that chamber. Following the 2012 election cycle, Republicans secured majorities in both chambers of the General Assembly. The difference in the partisan makeup of the House and the Senate between 2010 and 2014 highlights the sudden totality of GOP political gains in Arkansas government.

Term Limits and Open Seats

While the more recent GOP electoral success is the primary focus of this book, it is important to recall there were several causal elements that led to this sustained shift in partisanship in Arkansas, and these parts to the

Table 5.1

Arkansas General Assembly House and Senate Membership by Party, 1992–2020

Election Year	Senate Democrats	Republicans	House Democrats	Republicans
1992	30	5	89	10
1994	28	7	88	12
1996	28	6	86	14
1998	29	6	76	24
2000	27	8	72	28
2002	27	8	70	30
2004	27	8	72	28
2006	27	8	75	25
2008	27	8	71	28
2010	20	15	55	45
2012	14	21	49	51
2014	11	24	36	64
2016	9	26	27	73
2018	9	26	26	74
2020	7	28	22	78

Source: Gary D. Wekkin, "Arkansas: Electoral Competition and Reapportionment in the 'Land of Opportunity,'" in *The New Politics of the Old South: An Introduction to Southern Politics*, ed. Charles S. Bullock and Mark J. Rozell, 2nd ed. (New York: Rowman & Littlefield, 2003), 195–222; Arkansas Secretary of State, https://www.sos.arkansas.gov/elections/for-election-results.

puzzle, in many cases, occurred years—even decades—prior to the 2010s. In addition to the dynamics discussed in detail in previous chapters, term limits likely aided Republican's electoral efforts, particularly in the late 1990s. As outlined, 1992 functions as a divider between the first and second generations of the modern GOP in Arkansas. The reason for this is chiefly that the 1992 election cycle brought about momentous changes to the state's political landscape and the events that followed—many of which would not unveil their impact until years later—created both political disruption of the one-party Democratic dominance and opportunities for the GOP. In addition to Bill Clinton's presidential election—and the events following that dramatically altered the state's politics moving forward—Arkansas voters also opted into some of the strictest term limits on their state-level elected officials (and congressional-level elected officials, until the Supreme Court ruled the measure unconstitutional in *Thornton v. United States*). For a single-party-dominated state like Arkansas, term limits on state legislators created opportunities for the party out of power to compete in open seat elections. While the GOP would not gain majorities in the two chambers of the General Assembly until the 2010s, term limits—phased in over the years following their 1992 adoption—reduced the rate of incumbents seeking reelection and allowed the GOP to capitalize on a new political environment, albeit slowly. Of course, term limits altered state government beyond partisan politics—they dramatically changed the makeup of the state's legislative institutions. Recalling the impact term limits had on the General Assembly, longtime Arkansas House parliamentarian Tim Massanelli said:

> Well, the relationships among the members are nowhere near what they used to be, and simply because they don't have the time to develop them. You had people [who'd] been around you for fourteen years; they know you better than they did when you were there four years. And so those relationships between members have lessened. It is virtually impossible for a nonmember to come in there immediately and know and understand the whole process. It's too complicated. It's too diverse. It's just too many things. . . . So the members . . . fall short under term limits, if you will, in knowing the process—knowing what to do, not making mistakes and so forth. For example, one of the worst mistakes that a person can make over there is going down to the well of the House and talking the bill to death. See, those people over there, by and large, are educated. You don't have to hit them over the head with a hammer. They understand. Those bills have been through committee. They've read something about

> them in the press, and you don't need to go down there and do what we call overexplaining it.... You've got to know when to talk, and you've got to know when to shut up. And you have to develop that. There's no written piece of paper that tells you how you do it. You've got to feel it, and you got to know it, and you've got to know when to move out of there.... The minimum requirement is fifty-one votes, and it's not easy to muster up those kind of votes unless people have some kind of understanding of something that's going on.[3]

Additionally, former state senator, attorney general, and governor Mike Beebe—who, by virtue of timing, was the final legislator elected before term limits to be term-limited himself, shared his thoughts on how term limits impacted the state General Assembly and, more broadly, the political and partisan dynamics in Arkansas.

> I think term limits had a major effect. First of all, anecdotally, if you talk to people, "I didn't want to get rid of you. I tried to get rid of those folks in Washington when I voted for term limits." I mean, I heard that ad nauseam. I said, "Well, you didn't get rid of the folks in Washington, you got rid of me." And I had the best of both worlds. Politics from as high as you could go and be part-time. I still had a real job with real income; I had my own law firm. Yet I was deeply engaged in Arkansas politics and in public service to the point that I had the best of all . . . [I] might have stayed there forever.... And most senators only got eight years or half of them because of the way the redistricting works. I ended up with ten . . . but I was one of the last out the door. During that time you saw incumbents, who would most likely win, leave office and leave [their seat] open. And so you had a more competitive open seat situation in a lot of these districts, House districts and Senate districts. And that began a little bit of a rise of the number of Republicans. I think when I left, we had ten. I think we had three when I went into the Senate. So I mean, you just incrementally saw that. But it's still heavily Democratic. And it remained that way until 2010.[4]

As Governor Asa Hutchinson was also quoted as saying in an earlier chapter, open seat elections—free of the inherent advantages of incumbency—were key to Republicans becoming more competitive in contests in the 1990s and early 2000s. The state's strict term limits during that time likely aided the party's ability to recruit more viable candidates—an increasing proportion of whom, over time, gained office.[5]

The Rise of the GOP in Arkansas Government

As Table 5.1 illustrates, the 2010 election cycle was the series of contests that began to dramatically shift the political dynamics of the state. In the 1990s and early 2000s, the GOP's slow and steady pace of picking up seats—often open contests due to a term-limited incumbent—suggested that gaining majorities of positions in the Arkansas General Assembly was still years away. However, as discussed in previous chapters, a convergence of events led to 2010 and the following two cycles, the critical time for the GOP wave to overtake the state's politics.

As successful as 2010 was for Republicans in Arkansas, the GOP fell short of gaining the majority in either chamber of the General Assembly. The 2012 election cycle, and the following legislative session in January 2013, would result in the election of Davy Carter, the first GOP speaker of the Arkansas House of Representatives since Reconstruction. To provide an insider's account of election night and the weeks to follow, I interviewed Carter. This is what he had to say:

> Going into that election night, the Republican caucus thought that there could be as high as seventy-plus Republican seats. In fact, I would say that was kind of the expectation. So from the Democratic Party side, I think it turned out to be kind of a ... last great stand. Because when we woke up, the day after Election Day, there were fifty Republicans and one election was undecided, that ultimately was won by a Republican of Harrisburg. But they're fifty-one to forty-nine. And I remember getting a text message from Bill Vickery early the next day, [and he] said something like, "Hey, you know, Davy Carter, your vote becomes pretty important, there's fifty to fifty-one." And, you know, Bill was just being Bill, but it was excellent expectations were they to have a much, you know, greater majority. But nevertheless, there was still a majority.... Those next few months were pretty intense. I went into that election being pretty content with my career path—back then ... we were still kind of a part-time legislature. And there were people in the caucus that asked me to run for speaker before then; I just really didn't have the time to do it, honestly. I was honored to do it but didn't really ... want to do it. There were certainly some interesting days that occurred after the election with the organizational efforts of the caucus, and it was certainly a "new sheriff in town" attitude. There's no denying that. And I certainly was all for the policy changes that I felt needed to be made. But personally I wasn't too excited about getting into ... some of what we would refer to it as DC-type things.... One small group in the caucus, they wanted to remove Robert Moore

from the speaker's chair before it was traditionally done ... in January, and then there was an effort by some that wanted to make Beebe look as bad as possible, because he was so popular.... Things went downhill really quick in that regard, with some of our interpersonal relationships. And I remember one day, [I] called John Burris and a few others and said, "Let's meet and talk about this. I don't like the direction we're going in. I'm not going to be a part of part of that, and let's see what we can do differently." Going into the day of that election, I had no idea what was going to happen, and ... I don't know if that will ever happen again, but [it was] certainly dramatic.[6]

A GOP Speaker of the House— the 89th General Assembly

The 89th Arkansas General Assembly convened in January 2013. The House speaker was poised to be a member of the GOP for the first time since the nineteenth century. The speaker's race was complicated by the fact that the GOP held the chamber's majority seats by only the narrowest of margins. In the end, enough Republicans *and* Democrats supported Davy Carter's nomination. Carter, a banker representing a community in the central region of the state (Cabot), would not only be the first Republican speaker in 150 years, but a leader of the House whose party affiliation was different from that of the governor—another rarity given the state's one-party-dominated political history. Recalling his election as speaker, Carter said:

> I take pride in being a pragmatic, moderate person. But my voting record was pretty conservative.... I got sort of painted as [a centrist], but you know that really wasn't true.... The differences weren't so much about policy, although there were some organizational things that some of us didn't like about committee selections. Representative Williams was the speaker designate; he was a good friend of mine, a Democrat from Little Rock.... When he recognized that the votes [to elect a Democratic Speaker] weren't there, he gracefully stepped down.... I'm pretty sure all but one Democrat voted for me, and I'm proud of that.

The 2013 legislative session would stand out for another reason beyond the historic moment of a GOP speaker. A few years before, President Obama had signed the Patient Protection and Affordable Care Act (ACA). "Obamacare," as it was often called, was met with swift opposition from

Republicans across the country and the law seemed to have played a key role in the GOP's electoral successes in 2010 and 2012. Following its passage, the ACA was contested in court and a key provision in a Supreme Court ruling was poised to take a great deal of attention from the upcoming General Assembly. A narrow GOP majority in the legislature would have to work with a Democratic governor to navigate the issue and decide the fates of thousands of Arkansans' access to healthcare. Regarding the complexity and effort involved on this issue, Carter recalled:

At the time the GOP first gained legislative majorities in the General Assembly, the state's governor was Mike Beebe, a popular Democrat. Beebe had won his reelection bid handily in 2010 despite his party suffering major losses in virtually every other level of state and local government that cycle. This meant that the 2013 General Assembly was majority Republican while the governor was a Democrat. The defining issue of the legislative session would be related to the ACA. Recalling the pressures of the political environment and the likelihood of successfully addressing major policy issues with a divided government, Carter recalled:

> Yeah, well, I'll tell you the I never thought we would . . . if you really took time to evaluate the choices and the ramifications of the way the lawsuit was resolved. . . . We met in—this is true—a janitor's closet on the Senate end of the building, and we ended up having regular meetings there. And the first meeting [I said], "Look, I know every member has just run these races telling their constituents that they were, opposed to this. But we have a problem, and we have to fix the problem." . . . We just started working on it, we weren't going to just say no. . . . The easy thing politically would have been to stand up the first day and have some theatrics, talking about judicial activism and we could have disparaged the Supreme Court. . . . So hats off to the group that started the discussions with me . . . When we were in the janitor's closet, it was a learning process. . . . I think we were the first legislature to meet after that Supreme Court decision. Nobody in the country knew what the rules were . . . That's where relationships with Democratic colleagues, and, most importantly, Governor Beebe was important. I went to him and said, "Look, we're going to try. But will you help us ask for permission to do these things?" And he said, "Absolutely." He believed in it. And he believed just about everything that we ended up putting in the legislation. It was just common sense, generally conservative viewpoints on the subject. Had he not been governor, and had we not had those relationships—prior to being in that position—it would never have happened, because he was the one that had to go to President

Obama and his secretary of health and ask them for waivers for all the stuff we kept asking for.... And, to [Beebe's] credit, he could have stood there and yelled and screamed at us and gone on TV every night and talked about how the Republicans were holding back health care for Arkansans. It could have turned into what we see today so easily. But that's not the approach we took.... I'll give the entire membership credit. Even the ones that voted against it, they all took an incredible amount of time trying to learn what we were dealing with. It was an intense learning curve for everybody.[7]

Reflecting on the bipartisan effort to approach a polarizing issue such as Medicaid expansion in relationship to the ACA, Carter went on to say:

[Arkansas's ACA "private option"] would not happen today, there's no way. It's just the opposite.... I don't think people [today] put the effort in that some did then in trying to figure out the problem, that pragmatic approach. I don't see it much anywhere else either, not just here in Arkansas, but anywhere.

Asa Hutchinson and the GOP Supermajority

In 2014, Asa Hutchinson—the single most important figure for the success of the GOP in Arkansas—was elected governor. After decades of leading his party through the political wilderness, Hutchinson and his Republicans returned the state to a unified, one-party government—something with which the state was very familiar. However, this time, the single-party dominance stemmed from GOP control as Democrats began to find themselves in electoral freefall. While the 2013 legislative session's challenges were immense—as described earlier by Speaker Carter—the following years brought about their own challenges, as the GOP solely held the reins of government in Arkansas. The politics in the years leading up to this moment had become more nationalized and polarizing. A sizeable portion of the Arkansas voting pubic began to reject the notion of an Arkansas politics that was unique from other parts of the country. As the political brand of the GOP—consistent in message from the national to state and local levels—was adopted, the more nuanced Arkansas Democratic message remained associated with the party's national brand and issues, leading to wide rejection of Arkansas Democratic candidates.

The current political environment in Arkansas is much different from that of the past. The result is a majority party in the state that is much more ideologically cohesive than their Democratic predecessors. While the current climate might provide voters—and for that matter, the parties themselves—clarity in regard to the professed views of a candidate and how they might align with a particular party (gone are the days of conservative Democrats and liberal Republicans in Arkansas, or virtually anywhere for that matter), the pressure for ideological consistency and party discipline (new concepts in Arkansas politics) poses its own challenges. In the past, when electoral contests were settled in Democratic primaries, candidates would often focus on personality or hyperlocal political issues instead of ideological purity or party discipline, as the Democratic brand was simply the default vehicle for seeking office. Today, the same positions are settled in the GOP primary contests, but the focus of those contests are markedly different, as victory in Republican intraparty conflict often hinges on highlighting your conservative credentials (both on national and state issues) and convincing the voting public that between you and your opponent (also a Republican), you are the true conservative in the race. By pointing out this difference in focus and tone between what Arkansans saw from Democrats for decades and what we see today from Republicans is not to evaluate one as better than the other. A political space whereby virtually all Democrats are more progressive than not, and Republicans are likewise more conservative essentially simplifies the decision-making for voters—especially among an already more polarized electorate. However, these politics do introduce new pressures to governing for the majority party as primary voters assess an incumbent's fitness for another term based on how ideologically consistent they were in office. A sort of political arms race emerges as an incumbent's most significant threat to losing office comes in the form of a primary challenger who attempts to highlight any perceived space between you and the conservative ideal. The solution for the incumbent is to be as ideologically consistent as possible.

While primary challenges are not unusual, the notion that the only viable political threat to most Arkansas Republican incumbents is from another member of the same party is new to the GOP. In the past, Republican incumbents—more concerned about the Democratic opponent awaiting them in the General Election than an intraparty foe—would be wary of losing voters who still largely voted for Democrats. For example, Mike Huckabee—only the third GOP governor since Reconstruction—served as the state's executive for ten years at a time when Democrats still claimed significant majorities in both chambers of the Arkansas General Assembly, and faced foes from his own party who accused him of not pushing the state far enough into a more conservative direction. In 2001, when the chair of a conservative think tank in the state began to consider running against Huckabee in the GOP primary, he said to a reporter of the Republican incumbent governor's job performance, "That kind of leadership is not Republican in nature."[8] Here, Huckabee's potential primary challenger was questioning the incumbent Republican's commitment to a conservative agenda. The difference between then and today was Huckabee's response at a time when his party was in the minority and he had to court voters who voted for Democrats more often than not. In this instance, Huckabee rebutted his co-partisan critic by defending his brand of conservative pragmatism, saying, "Most Republicans know how hard it was for us to get some of the positions we now hold, how hard we worked to be here. . . . Most of those folks, the people who sit down and think about it, aren't going to want to throw out an incumbent Republican and nominate someone they're not sure can relate to the everyday voter when it comes November [2002]." Huckabee was a conservative by all accounts, but his effectiveness as a governor stemmed largely from his ability and willingness to work with Republicans and Democrats alike. He openly mocked members of his own party who refused to support bipartisan initiatives to raise state revenues or who otherwise held a more hardline conservative stance, calling them "Shiite Republicans."[9] Huckabee's tactics in answering critiques from within his own party in the early 2000s were appeals to the state's split-ticket voter as much as they were rebukes to challengers from his political right. Today, it is hard to imagine the same response in a political climate where a Republican incumbent must often remain more vigilant for challenges from within their own party than attacks volleyed by Democrats.

The approach to lead the state in a way that reflected conservative ideology while also exhibiting a brand of pragmatism with which Arkansans had long grown accustomed extended into the third generation of the GOP and the election of Hutchinson as governor, who, unlike Huckabee, had majorities in both legislative chambers when he took office in 2015. Recalling when the GOP—having just become the dominant party—was feeling out the role of majority party, and the transition to today, where Arkansas is one of the most Republican states in the country, longtime columnist John Brummett said:

> Hutchinson, and Republicans like Davy Carter, who was speaker of the House, were practical, moderate fellows. . . . I remember Carter visiting with me and saying, "We've got to show we can govern. Now, we've got to

govern." And I think there was that practical consideration of conservative but not extreme ideological Republicans.... And for a while [Hutchinson] as governor could see some of these culturally conservative bills percolating while Representative So-and-So [was] getting ready to put in a transgender bathroom bill or something like that. And he could lean on that person—I saw this happen—"Don't do it. We've got to show we can govern, and if we invite national boycotts or national problems, it's the worst thing we can do. This [is] not the time for this. We've got to tend to the sort of Walmart conservatism . . . and we've got to continue this moderation and modernization theme that began in '66." And he could stop it. That happened for a while, and I was able to cover this legislature and think, "This isn't terribly different from what I've long covered."[10]

Despite the similarities in the pragmatic styles between Democratic and Republican governance Brummett had witnessed as a journalist over the years, he also remarked on recent changes he's seen from the GOP since the party gained supermajorities in the General Assembly and have continued to grow in virtually every level of government in Arkansas:

The cultural conservatives, or movement conservatives, said, "[To] hell with it, we've waited long enough, we've shown we can govern. Now let's do what we want." And there is this pent-up frustration: "We're not going to have any abortion. We're going to have 'stand your ground.' We're going to teach Creationism in the schools, whatever we want. It's our time because we've played your game, Asa [Hutchinson], we've played your game, Davy Carter. We're sure we can govern. We can pass appropriation bills; we can keep this thing afloat. But it's time to do what we believe in."[11]

The belief that the nature of intraparty pressure has recently changed within the Republican Party in Arkansas is shared by Carter. When asked whether the work of the 2013 General Assembly to expand Medicaid in Arkansas—with a Democratic governor and GOP speaker—could happen today, his response was:

Zero percent chance. It would never happen. . . . I do think the national groups are more vocal, and social media is more present. . . . I'm not being negative about the current members of the General Assembly, I just think it's a completely different environment. . . . Doing the private option and writing that legislation was for the best for the people of Arkansas, [I] sincerely believe that. I also knew that it was very difficult to explain to the base. But notwithstanding . . . we carried on anyway, not considering our own political futures or the ramifications. . . . I didn't make a lot of friends with the Republican base donors, but I'm not stupid, I knew that it was still the right thing to do. . . . They're under so much more pressure now, with the DC stuff taking over the dialogue, and I hear routinely how there are members who are [voting] for things or not voting for things but it's not really what they want to do, but they feel—they know—they don't really have a choice. I remember someone came to see me in the speaker's office during the [ACA discussions. He said:] "Look, I campaigned against this heavily. I know and you know that voting for this is the right thing to do. But I can't do it. I campaigned against it. And I can't explain to my constituents why I would do it." [I replied,] "There are no free passes here; we're all in that position, but sometimes you've got to step up to the plate."

On the topic of navigating a divided government (as he did in the final years of his second term) former governor Beebe, the last Democrat to win a statewide race for the foreseeable future, said:

It wasn't any different for me, working with Republicans in the General Assembly as governor versus Democrats. There were jerks on the Democratic side and jerks on the Republican side. There were allies on the Democratic side and allies on the Republican side. There are reasonable people on both sides and the crazies exist, if you will, on both sides. And I think Asa Hutchinson will tell you this to this day, sometimes he has more trouble working with his own party than he does with the opposite party.[12]

On the same topic of what intraparty competition in a one-party GOP state might look like moving forward, Governor Hutchinson explained:

It's going to be contested primaries, it's going to be competition, to win the next office or position yourself for it. And we see that now, the hotly contested races are going to be on the Republican side in the upcoming elections, for both lieutenant governor and attorney general, you've got different candidates. One of the reasons [the Democrats] lost the majority is philosophy and national politics. The other is that they built their party and continue to strengthen it based upon personalities . . . versus the structure of the party. [By] the time we took over, we had strong county committees, people were committed, we had women's clubs, and they were much stronger than on the Democratic side. For me, the test of the Republican Party is—sure, we're going to have dominant personalities, we're going to have contested primaries, but you cannot lose the framework of elections and party structure and the importance of that. And that is the biggest risk to the Republican Party, that we continue to strengthen that. And we do not just simply let that go to the most extreme elements of our party. We have to be a party of ideas, we have to debate ideas. And we cannot simply become ideologues in our party structure. That will weaken it over time.[13]

Changes in Policy and Governing

While Arkansas has historically been one of the most solidly Democratic states in the country, it has never been considered particularly progressive or liberal. As discussed earlier in this book, the Democratic brand was pragmatic and localized, steeped in generational loyalties, based on personalities, and—ideologically—moderate- to conservative-leaning. Given this history, the transition from a one-party-dominated Democratic government to a one-party-dominated GOP government has not resulted in dramatically different policy at a wholesale level in the state. However, there is no doubt that policy implemented in the state today is more consistently conservative under GOP leadership. Governor Hutchinson summarized the shift in policy that began when he was sworn into office:

> [There are] significant differences between Democratic governance and Republican governance at the state level. I came in in 2015, the first time in history that we had Republicans control both the House [and] Senate General Assembly, as well as the governorship. It was almost startling to understand what had not been done in the past. For example, every year for one hundred years, our department of finance would forecast what the revenues would be. And then every dime of that would be budgeted and spent. That happened for one hundred years. And you had to scratch your head and say, "Well, where's our savings account? Where's our reserve fund?" Other states had built up reserve funds to weather an economic downturn, but we hadn't. Under Republican governance, we started building that savings account that has grown to over half a billion dollars now, and which helps in bond ratings. And that had not been done for one hundred years. The income tax in Arkansas had moved up to a 7 percent level under Democratic leadership. For the first time in history, under Republican leadership we started lowering it. And it's now been lowered from 7 percent down to 5.9 percent. And there's a unity of opinion that we need to do more. Not only a shift in historic directions, but

also in terms of the structure of government itself. The Democratic Party and its leadership saw that as plum assignments. Let's put everybody who worked in a political campaign in government employment somewhere ... under Republican leadership, we've reduced state employment by over fifteen hundred employees. And that's [at] a time our state is growing. Our services expand, but state agency employees have been decreased. The mindset of the executive officers that lead these agencies is: "How can you save money? How can you do things more efficiently?" That had never been discussed and preached and made an integral part of governing. So those are just a couple of differences. Obviously, we pass a lot more conservative legislation in terms of regulations and pro-life. But fundamentally, those things I point to are the reduction in taxes, an increased savings account, a reduction in state employment, those are fundamental differences.[14]

Jay Barth, political scientist and Arkansas politics scholar, summarized what he has witnessed in terms of policymaking trends over the years, extending into the period since the GOP became the dominant party in Arkansas today:

What we tended to see was basically pragmatism, in that the focus was on getting the job done, rather than ideology. The first [initiative was] the private option, the expansion of Medicaid; that's the classic example and it was not ideological. There was some ideological opposition to it. But the focus was on, "Let's overcome that and still get health care for Arkansans." An aspect of pragmatism was trying to avoid some of these social issues that became a distraction from getting the job done on these bread-and-butter issues. Arkansas didn't have much immigration legislation that passed in either direction ... rarely had abortion legislation passed—it was often introduced, but it didn't get through. Aside from the ban on same-sex marriage in the [state] constitution, there wasn't a lot of legislation. There were things that were introduced that were never dealt with, because they were seen as too distracting from the pragmatic work of the government. I think we've reached a point where some of this old pragmatism remains and hasn't gone away, because now it's just as essential to the fundamentals of governance and balancing a budget. But now there's so much more attention on [divisive social] issues, which I think really distract and divert from the core pragmatism of the state that had been in place for decades. That's the fundamental change. And it's the question is if we'll reach a point where the desire to make points on social issues starts to fundamentally break some these commitments that have been made through these pragmatic compromises and that's the grand question: "Does ideological purity ever reach a point where it starts to break government apart?" We haven't gotten there yet. These things are certainly deeply painful to folks who were and are affected by the legislation, but we are not at a point where they can completely decimate core programs on education, health care, and other things that have been made over the decades.[15]

No matter one's partisan or ideological leanings or view on the impacts of contemporary conservative policymaking, it would be difficult to dispute that the GOP in Arkansas, in its current form, is more consistent in its brand, messaging, and governmental philosophy than Democrats were in their years of power. Only time will tell the overall long-term impacts of the dramatic political shifts the state has seen regarding public policy, but the short-term impact marks a noted shift to more conservative policy outputs.

According to the American Conservative Union's (ACU) Center for Legislative Accountability (CLA), the Arkansas General Assembly's policymaking has become one of the most conservative state legislative branches in the country.[16] The ACU is one of the leading conservative advocacy political organizations in the United States and has been assessing and publishing congressional voting scores (offering a measure of conservatism based on a sampling of roll-call votes from member's voting records) for fifty years. More recently, the CLA has begun to publish scores on overall legislative chambers at the state level. The rankings for Arkansas's General Assembly from 2013 to 2019 can be found in Table 5.2.

Table 5.2

Center for Legislative Accountability Scores for the Arkansas General Assembly

Year	Ranking	Year	Ranking
2013	10th	2017	20th
2015	8th	2018*	3rd
2016	27th*	2019	2nd

Note: * denotes a fiscal session, as the Arkansas General Assembly meets every even year for a regular legislative session.

The ACU's Center for Legislative Accountability does not report a score for each calendar year for Arkansas. The Arkansas General Assembly meets every other year (odd years) to consider a wide span of legislative issues. The legislative branch meets every even year for a fiscal session in which the assembly is narrowly focused on budgetary issues. General session scores indicate a broader array of bills. Fiscal session bills are few and strictly surround budgetary approval, unless a special session is called or an overwhelming majority of members seek to add something else to the agenda for consideration. While the Table 5.2 data is limited to a span of only six years, the more recent sessions have resulted in the General Assembly becoming more conservative relative to other states' legislative branches.

Based on firsthand accounts, quantitative data, and a bit of common sense, it is obvious that the state's government—never known as a liberal bastion despite its long history of being comprised primarily of Democrats—has become more conservative as it has become more Republican. As the GOP has gained ground in Arkansas, its base has become emboldened and has endeavored to push elected officials to more contemporary conservative positions, particularly on social issues and other policies that reflect the nationalized politics of the day, a departure from what the state has seen in the past. This recent trend is likely to continue, as the GOP appears to be poised to control most governmental apparatuses in the state for years to come.

One Party Rule: An Arkansas Tradition

Arkansas is not new to one-party rule, but one-party dominance in Arkansas today does not look much like the one-party dominance of the past. Beyond the difference of the party in the driver's seat, the party in power today operates from a more ideological perspective—reflecting the GOP's top-down (national to state) brand consistency discussed in previous chapters. While some divisions might exist today among personality or regional lines, most intraparty factions and conflicts appear to be emerging among ideological and policy lines—a key departure from the past. In other words, the factions among the ruling party in today's state government are primarily divided about what it means to be conservative and, once a prevailing decision is made, divided over what degree of conservatism GOP elected officials believe a policy or group of policies should be. The rivalries, at this point, are primarily philosophical with previous culprits of in-party fighting—also witnessed at the hands of Democrats—largely, if only for now, thrust into the background.

What will one-party rule by Republicans mean for Arkansas? While the state has previously seen a single party dominate virtually all levels of governmental power a comparison of the era in which V. O. Key Jr. wrote with today's environment would be misleading. Key's observations, made several decades ago about an aimless ruling class merely sharing a common label without regard to ideology or clear policy goals, do not match well with the politics of the state today. For one, the GOP now has clear ideological and policy goals and—unlike the Democrats of yesteryear—the Republicans align their brand perfectly with their party's national presence. Second—and this is more of an artifact of the 1970s to early 2000—Arkansas voters no longer ticket-split, allowing little space for candidates to carve out niches apart from within their own partisan primaries. According to the Arkansas Poll, only a small portion of the Arkansas population currently identifies as liberal—or ever has, for that matter.[17] The art of a well-known, liked, and trusted candidate finessing the distance between their own views, the views of their more conservative constituents, and their more liberal national party is no longer permitted. Gone is the license for a popular incumbent to move within their own political space. One-party dominance today, with the GOP at the helm, has and will result in a strident conservative policy direction. So, while regional factions and personal rivalries may exist today within the GOP (as they did in the day of Key's assessments of the state's politics decades ago), these issues are largely overcome by agreements about policy and ideology.

6

CONCLUSION

No single event or individual can explain the historic shift from Democratic Party dominance to one-party Republican rule in Arkansas. As illustrated in the previous chapters, what occurred seemingly overnight was years—if not decades—in the making. I have examined the historic rise of the GOP in Arkansas in the context of three generations of the modern Republican Party in the state, spanning nearly seven decades. I have also modeled a study on the three parts of a political party in the manner of V. O. Key Jr.: the party in the electorate, the party organization, and the party in government. After introducing the current state of politics in Arkansas and the historic partisan shift that has occurred in chapter 1, I framed the modern era of the GOP around three distinct generations in chapter 2. In chapter 3, I assessed the events and changes in behavior among the electorate through the years, as the state shifted from Democratic to Republican control. A study on the Democratic and Republican Party state organizations was the focus of chapter 4. There, I concluded that a stronger GOP party apparatus emerges between the late 1990s and 2010s—a pivotal period for the party in the state. Chapter 5 addressed the ways in which the shift in partisanship has affected state government. It is my hope that together these chapters illuminate the myriad factors that, over decades, led to the change in party control in Arkansas.

The modern GOP can trace its roots to the election of Winthrop Rockefeller in 1966. Ironically, as Rockefeller became the first Republican governor in Arkansas since Reconstruction, his progressive blend of politics was losing favor in his party; the contemporary GOP was already becoming more uniformly conservative. Rockefeller's electoral success—based largely on his ability to build a broad coalition of reformers and others fatigued by the politics of the Faubus era—was short-lived. The GOP he attempted to build in Arkansas in the 1960s would move rightward in the years to come and—while the state party's headquarters bears his name—it is hard to imagine that his brand of politics would resonate well with GOP primary voters today. Nevertheless, Rockefeller's political success, along with Congressman John Paul Hammerschmidt, showed that Arkansas voters would support Republican candidates if conditions were right. The first generation sees the state's partisan politics operate in much the same way until the early 1990s. Democrats are the overwhelming default party, but Arkansans—on rare occasion—would vote for a Republican in state or local races.

The biggest shift in the state's politics during this time occurs at the top of the ticket, as a plurality of Arkansas voters begin to support GOP presidential candidates. This behavior exhibited an independent streak among Arkansas voters and illustrated their rejection of more liberal national Democratic politics. However, the state's voters continued to overwhelmingly support down-ticket Democrats. Arkansas voters (and not just Democrats) made a distinction between the national Democratic brand and the state's Democratic brand. Many voters seemed to communicate at the ballot box that moderate to relatively progressive politics were palpable if they knew and trusted the candidate. This served many Arkansas Democrats well—particularly those whose personal connections to voters seemed to extend beyond their political party, such as Dale Bumpers, David Pryor, Bill Clinton, and later Mike Beebe.

The 1992 election proved to be a pivotal time in the state's partisan politics and a key cutoff point between the first and second generations of the GOP in the state. With Clinton's election as president of the United States, the political vacuum his ascendance to the White House created, as well as the eventual political fallout of his replacement—Jim Guy Tucker—all meant that the second generation of the modern Republican Party was far more promising than the first. While the GOP did not see the political gains fellow Republican peers saw in other southern states, the 1990s and early 2000s were a time of significant change that led to a party that would one day be capable of not only winning more elections but also maintaining an enduring level of dominance in Arkansas. From Mike Huckabee serving as governor for over ten years and key congressional contest victories, to successful legal challenges to the state's outdated electoral practices and enhancements to the state's party organization, the second generation—from 1993 to 2010—laid the groundwork for the way the party positions itself through the 2020s.

The third generation of the modern GOP in Arkansas begins in 2010 and continues today. Currently, Republicans dominate most facets of partisan politics in Arkansas. It is an era in which former state GOP chair Doyle Webb, when speaking at the 2020 Republican National Convention, suggested "Arkansas is the most Republican state in the US"—and meant it. While there are still some elected officials, party activists, and party officials whose public life extends over the two previous generations of the party, growing numbers of Republican—and Democratic for that matter—politicos have only operated in a political space where the GOP is the majority party. This political form of generational replacement in Arkansas is most prevalent in GOP primary contests and in—often public—critiques and accusations of "RINOs" (Republicans in name only). The litmus test for a "conservative Republican" seems to keep moving farther to the right. In a state where General Elections are becoming once again a mere formality, an ideological purity—once largely absent in the days of one-party Democratic rule—has emerged in the majority party's infighting and campaigning.

This intergenerational rivalry within the GOP indicates a division within the party— between those who know what it was like to operate in a state where their party was on the outside looking in on a one-party state and those whose relative newness to the politics of Arkansas stems from never knowing a loss. In this new environment, no one is immune from public infighting. For example, members of his own party regularly assail Asa Hutchinson, a former congressman, party chairperson, and only the fourth Republican governor since the nineteenth century. It was Hutchinson who ran and lost numerous times running as a Republican in the 1980s and 1990s before leading his party organization, winning a seat in the US House of Representatives, and later becoming the first GOP governor with successive supermajorities of his party in the General Assembly. Now, he is publicly chastised by members of his party (including former president Donald Trump) as lacking conservative Republican credentials—events once seen as incredulous.[1]

Political disputes within a party are to be expected. However, infighting does come with risks—even to the party in power. When asked about the challenges the GOP faces today, Dr. Hal Bass, professor emeritus of political science at Ouachita Baptist University, considered intraparty conflict as the primary risk to the current strength of the GOP in Arkansas.

When asked what the state's Republican Party must do to maintain its advantage, Bass said:

> I'm a whole lot better [at] looking back than I am [at] looking forward. . . . But I think in the immediate short run, simply avoiding intraparty divisions, and not getting caught up in civil wars. I think conflict is inherent in human interaction. And if it's not occurring between the parties, it's going to occur within the dominant party. . . . But [it's important to] manage the tensions and try to hold together what is ultimately a coalition here. There are some strong national forces that are helping the Republicans at this point that do resonate well in Arkansas. But if you're going to have a majority in a state with three million inhabitants, you're going to have to manage some diversity there. And whether it's regional, whether it's personalistic, whether its ecological, whether it's issues, something will come up that will prove divisive. And the question is, how effective will the Republicans be in papering over those divisions, and what's helped them is being able to demonize Democrats. A weakened Democratic Party is harder to demonize.[2]

Despite intraparty conflict, the GOP has continued to improve its position within the state. The GOP had already claimed historic gains before Donald Trump announced his presidential candidacy in 2015. Despite some trepidation from the state's most prominent Republican officeholders, Trump won the state's GOP delegates for the nomination in 2016.[3] In Arkansas, Trump's brand of populist politics was met with open arms from a majority of the state's general election voters in 2016—despite his opponent (former secretary of state Hillary Clinton) having strong ties to the state. He went on to win the state again in 2020—as the GOP also expanded their representation in the General Assembly.[4]

Trump was either a catalyst for or byproduct of a shift in priorities, stances, and political stylings within the GOP at the national level, and his tenure in office altered the intraparty dynamics within the state. A sizeable portion of Arkansas voters were highly supportive of President Trump while he was in office.[5] In him, they found a message that has resonated with Natural State voters in the past. While it might be difficult to expect the appeal of Trump—a wealthy New Yorker who, on paper, has very little in common with the average Arkansan—sizeable portions of Arkansas voters have been drawn to populist appeals before Trump. In 1968, a plurality of Arkansas voters supported the third-party presidential candidacy of populist and segregationist George Wallace of Alabama. Later, in 1990, the increase in GOP turnout in the state's GOP gubernatorial primary was at least, in part, due to the appeal of the bombastic populism of Tommy Robinson. If past behavior is any indication, it is likely that large numbers of Arkansans will continue to support a message similar to Trump's and those before his, even after he leaves the political arena.

Asa Hutchinson: The Architect of the Modern GOP in Arkansas

Throughout the period covered in this book, there is one constant over the last several decades regarding the struggles and eventual successes of the GOP in Arkansas. If there is one person who connects the multiple variables that have led to the state's current partisan environment, it is Governor Asa Hutchinson. He is the architect of key party initiatives and strategies that positioned Republicans to eventually seize opportunities and sustain the gains they have captured over the last two decades. From running in political contests with no real hope to succeed (save to have the party represented on the ballot), to recruiting Mike Huckabee to run in a 1993 special election for lieutenant governor; from challenging the legality of election processes in the state that significantly disadvantaged the GOP, to contrasting the brands of the two parties in order to appeal to conservatives who had long split their votes, advantaging state and local Democrats; and finally, to serving as the first Republican governor in this new era of GOP dominance in the state—it is safe to say that no person has played a larger role in the party's success. Only time will tell if Hutchinson's brand of conservatism will win out over his intraparty rivals' views.

Today, Arkansas is in the midst of a new political era. In addition to Republicans thriving in this once Solid South Democratic state, its parochial political traditions are being challenged. The nationalization of partisan politics, as I have stated in earlier chapters, has illustrated distinctions between the two major national parties and—as the parties have adopted more consistent messages and brands—broken down any perceived differences between partisans in Arkansas and any other state. Republicans know this brand consistency is essential to their continued electoral success in Arkansas. Remarking on this topic, former US representative, lieutenant governor, and current attorney general Tim Griffin said:

> I talk a lot about brand confusion. . . . People won't know why you're different. You say you're different. You've got a different platform. Would you raise taxes as much as the Democrats? How are you different? That's not good . . . we're separate parties because we have different views and values, but if parties start to adopt the views and values of each other in a way that confuses things, then it I don't think that's healthy.[6]

This brand consistency has greatly advantaged Republicans in Arkansas as those more conservative voters who had previously split their tickets are now voting more consistently Republican. The result is a Democratic Party that is struggling to articulate a message that resonates with the large portion of conservative white, rural (and suburban) voters of Arkansas and a Republican Party that fully embraces a more nationalized politics. For example, President Trump's former press secretary and the daughter of Governor Huckabee, Sarah Huckabee Sanders, announced her candidacy for governor of Arkansas in 2021 and immediately became the field favorite to win the GOP nomination and general election in 2022. She went on to win the 2022 race by a similar margin to Trump's in the state in 2020. When speaking about the issue of nationalized messaging to supporters at an event in Cabot in the fall of 2021, Sanders replied, "As I travel around the state, I keep hearing this criticism, 'Oh, there's that Sarah Sanders, nationalizing the race.' And my answer to those people is, 'You bet I am.' Because if you're not paying attention to what is happening in this country, you're missing what is going on."[7] Governor Huckabee Sanders embodies the future of the Republican Party in Arkansas. Her talents have also been recognized by her party outside of Arkansas, as she gave the Republican Party response to President Joe Biden's 2023 State of the Union address—a prominent stage that doubtlessly enhanced her standing as a possible future GOP candidate for national office. Her political style, use of social media, and adoption of national cultural issues in her legislative agenda appeal to Republicans and seem a good match for the current political environment in the state. She and others in the third generation of the GOP are not only changing politics and policy in Arkansas, but also the scope of topics of campaigns in a state that still values personal contact and retail politics, albeit now immersed in nationalized issues and media.

The Future of Partisan Politics in Arkansas

Eventually, anyone pondering the recent shift in Arkansas politics will arrive at the question: *What's next*? Based on the current political landscape, it would be hard to be anything but bullish about the short-term future of the GOP in Arkansas. The party has not only maintained its position as the predominant party of the last decade, but also continues to expand its breadth in state legislative and local races. The duration of the current political environment is the bigger puzzle. Parties and political environments change. When conducting interviews for this project on behalf of the David and Barbara Pryor Center for Arkansas Oral and Visual History, I asked Arkansas politicos, scholars, and reporters what the partisan future for Arkansas held. Dr. Jay Barth, M. E. and Ima Graves Peace Distinguished Emeritus Professor of Politics at Hendrix College and director of the William J. Clinton Presidential Library and Museum, reflected on the generational impact he has seen among young, politically ambitious professionals—the lifeblood for the future of partisan politics in Arkansas:

> We tend to focus so much on the voters . . . the voters are the customers in the process of buying [a] candidate, buying between choices that are kind of sitting up on the political shelf here. But we've got to focus on the products that are being offered. And I think historically, there was such a gap in terms of the quality of the products, the Democrats just had much stronger candidates than Republicans. Over time, though, we really started to see a reshaping of that, and eighteen, nineteen, twenty-somethings who say, "I want to be involved in public life now." Unless they are in a couple of places in the state, it really makes no sense for them to run as Democrats. And so they have a choice. If they are committed to the values of the Democratic Party, they've either got to move to one of those neighborhoods where they can still win, or they get out of state, or they just give up on that desire to serve in public life. Or, if they are more ideologically malleable, the place to go is the Republican Party. And I think that's the change that has taken place that is important and will have generational ramifications. Even if we have another swing back ten years from now, there's going to be a candidate quality gap, but the candidate quality gap will not be in the Democrats' favor . . . it'll be in the Republicans' favor. If you went to a law school class at Fayetteville fifteen years ago, those folks who were thinking about running for office were going to run as Democrats. Now, you go into that same class, and those same folks—who may not be all that different ideologically than [fifteen

years ago]—they're going to run us as Republican, because that's really their only option. We need to think about candidate quality and how that change is occurring, and how it has lasting ramifications. As we saw for the Democrats, they had a big advantage . . . because the quality of their candidates was so much stronger for so long.

Indeed, for decades, one hurdle for the GOP in the state was that Democratic Party affiliation was seen as the only way to succeed in state politics. In the past, a young, politically ambitious individual would have seen running as a Democrat as the default (and often, only viable) position. Now, as Barth points out, that has changed. The dramatic shift we have seen has also likely impacted the way in which future office seekers perceive political viability and political parties in Arkansas—advantaging the GOP in much the same way Democrats had previously benefited for generations.

When tasked with predicting the future of the state's partisan balance, Dr. Angie Maxwell, associate professor of political science and director of the Diane D. Blair Center for Southern Politics and Society, reflected on the challenges of governing and the risks associated with the dominant party becoming too ideologically pure:

[The GOP, after decades of being the minority party] have been on the offense. . . . I'm watching redistricting [happen] right now. They've never done it, not since Reconstruction. It's complicated, and there are things coming that people don't see. And there are consequences. They've never done it [before]. It's not because they're dumb or they don't pay attention. It's because they have never done it. That is strange. A lot of the other Southern states, they flipped but they had a back and forth for a while. They had a period of time where they had to work together, or they had oversight like they wanted. They couldn't go spike the football because they lost the next cycle. That's not what happened in Arkansas. It just went and totally flipped so dramatically. We didn't get that middle period. We don't have best practices for how to do that. We have some executives that [know how], but we don't have a legislature that [does]. That is a huge challenge right now, and it's unique to Arkansas. It's part of that effect of the long-term Southern Strategy and . . . why it delayed in Arkansas. When it came, it's like the floodwaters were held back. Why [it] was in sync with the national moment, and it happened so fast. And wild. Now we're saying, "Whoa, we've got to build a bench on the

Democratic side and build infrastructure on the Republican side. We got to learn cooperation and party priorities, and not just this crazy . . . 'We'll sue the governor, we run everything, compromise is a dirty word,'" [attitude]. That happens when you assume the majority quickly and it's all you've ever known, and the national brand is supporting it. All those factors lined up in Arkansas. And I think there are a whole lot of people somewhere in the middle, who are kind of conservative to moderate . . . that need the extremes to find this common ground and middle. But we'll see what happens.[8]

Interviewed in the fall of 2020, Rex Nelson, former advisor to Governor Huckabee and longtime journalist, believed, like Maxwell, that the future of the state's politics was in the hands of the GOP and relied upon how they managed the moment.

[The future] depends on what the Republican Party does. If the Republican Party makes a hard right turn, I think that opens the door for some Democratic comeback in Arkansas. I note, we have a growing Hispanic population in Arkansas. Those kids now will vote eventually, and the voting numbers among Hispanics will go up. We have a lot of new people moving to Arkansas, particularly Northwest Arkansas, with the growth of that economy and the fact it's become one of the most desirable places to live in America. A lot of those people come from urban Democratic areas and tend to be Democratic voters. So if the Republicans make this hard right turn, they go away from the pragmatism we've seen in Asa Hutchinson and Mike Huckabee, it opens the door for Democrats to make a comeback. However, we remain real pragmatic with a Rockefeller/Huckabee/Hutchinson style of governing in Arkansas, I think it'll be very hard for the Democrats, even over a ten- to twenty-year period. That being said, I'm firmly convinced because of where the state is now that we're going to elect a Republican as governor of Arkansas in 2022. But what kind of Republican is it going to be? In that sense, I think that the Republican primary for governor in 2022 is one of the most important elections of our lifetime in Arkansas.[9]

Similarly, Dr. Janine A. Parry, university professor of political science at the University of Arkansas and director of the Arkansas Poll, specified the roles and responsibilities of the up-and-coming GOP political players in constructing the future for the state's politics:

I suspect that it hinges on Sarah Huckabee Sanders's inevitable governorship and what kind of governor she chooses to be. . . . We're in the midst of this nationalization of messaging that has now completely subsumed state politics everywhere—not just in Arkansas, but especially in Arkansas, where we don't have high levels of income and education. We don't have a big urban center to work as any kind of counterweight, whatever direction the majority of the voters are going. They go all-in right. So we're back to a one-party-ism that's so one-party-ism, it's almost no-party-ism. And we're back to this personalism—I say "back to," but maybe we never really left it. But it seems to me that our affinity for Trump, and being one of these states that was just all in, shouldn't have surprised any of us who've watched Arkansas politics for a long time. . . . I think it all hinges on what happens with [Sanders] and whether she stays for a long time or moves up into the national stage, which I think is clearly among her goals, but she's got plenty of time for that. And which direction she tries to lead because she's got that Trump brand. She's an heir apparent in that way. I think being a native Arkansan and sounding right and looking right and now having the brands right, that's also correct for this time period. It's hers to direct, that personality-based stuff, much [like] it did for her dad and made him a long-lived and really quite successful governor . . . I think the future of the Republican Party and future Republican candidates perhaps isn't really as much about the party in a weird way. It's wholly about the party and yet not wholly about the party. It also has a lot to do with her as its vessel, because I think that personalism is still a part of it. I could be wrong, as party's swamping everything else. And the Trump thing was just a short-lived Trump thing. I'm curious to see to see how that unfolds, and what kind of leader she'll be. Everything I'm hearing . . . is that she's just magnetic in person. She has all the credentials in this environment to do really well, but she also just really connects with people.[10]

Reflecting on how Arkansas was the last southern state to move solidly Republican, and how the state will likely also be the last southern state to once again become a two-party competitive environment (let alone Democratic), Parry continued:

Hal Holbrook said, "When the world ends, I want to be in Arkansas, because everything here happens twenty years later." So some of those southern states with big metropolitan areas will flip. And those will become competitive, I think, for the foreseeable future. Because [some think in terms of] south versus north, or coasts versus inland. But it's really rural versus urban. And then the suburbs are the swingers. . . . It was a little frustrating in 2018 and 2020. We're armchair analysts on Facebook, who almost always have PhDs in areas that are not political science. We're talking about how Arkansas could be the next Georgia, if we could only register enough people, and this kind of thing. But it's wishful thinking; you'd have to have an Atlanta. What's happening in Georgia [would not be happening] without Stacey Abrams. And it turns out that not everyone [understands this]. So when it happens, I think it will be in Northwest Arkansas. But it might not be for twenty years, it might not be for forty years. . . . It's going to take a really long time. And the parties could be totally reconfigured at that point, because I think we're in a period of realignment—we have a party that's crumbling and grasping at straws. And that's a very strange thing to say when they have trifecta control of two-thirds or three-quarters of the states. But nobody cares about that . . . it's a party that is in the death rattles. It's a very slow-moving, labored breathing. But they're either going to have to reconfigure or a new party system is going to rise, right? Maybe it'll come from that reconfiguring; so who knows, by the time Arkansas changes, the whole national landscape may have changed.[11]

Among those asked, Governor Beebe—to date, the last Democrat to win a statewide contest—provided a unique, more philosophical perspective. In his years in politics, Beebe operated in both unified and divided governments and was—and still is—respected and admired by those he has worked with and served, regardless of their party affiliation. Perhaps due to his firsthand experience, he is led to believe the rise to prominence of the GOP that is currently underway is not an indication of another century of single-party dominance, but of a political back-and-forth between the two competing parties and the state's voters. Sharing his opinion on the future of politics in the state, Beebe stated:

All this stuff is cyclical: life [is] cyclical, certainly politics are cyclical. You see the pendulum swing one way, but it will swing back. I don't know if it'll ever swing to the point where it's heavily Democratic, it [will] probably swing to the point where it's more in the middle, where it's more a fifty-fifty sort of thing. When will that be? I don't know. To a large extent, it'll be dependent on personalities. Trump is an example of that . . . he said, "I could shoot somebody on Fifth Avenue, and my people would still be winning." . . . The cult of personality plays a major role in the rise or fall of political prominence, and to some extent, political parties. Well, you're seeing a backlash, even in the Republican Party. But it's not a strong enough division yet for the Republicans to abandon Trump. So what's going on? Well, you're seeing a closer contraction of people coming more toward the middle. They don't like AOC, Elizabeth Warren, and some of the more liberal policies, and they don't like the far right. A lot of them are fed up with Trump. There's a compression of folks back toward the middle. That's the cyclical nature of politics. And that's the cyclical nature of what we can expect to see. When will it happen? I have no clue. It's not going to be tomorrow. It's not going to be in the next year or two. But it's gradually going to occur. And you look at what other states have done: North Carolina has gone from deep, deep red, to really purple. Texas came close to electing a Democratic senator against an incumbent in the last election; Texas is moving more purple. So while we were "late to the party" to go Republican in Arkansas, we're going to be late to the party to go back purple.[12]

Are Democrats in the 2020s in as bad a shape as the GOP was in those early years of its modern era? Are we now witnessing a repeat of Arkansas history where the players are different, the party power dynamics are opposite, but with the basic elements the same? As discussed previously in the book, there was a time—particularly, in the first generation of the modern GOP, when the party's only apparent hope for winning a statewide or otherwise highly visible contest in Arkansas was for the Democrats to commit a strategic error. For example, at least part of Rockefeller's electoral success stemmed from Democrats' reluctance to move past the Orval Faubus era of the 1950s and early 1960s, resulting in enough voters seeking change from the status quo to elect a Republican to the statehouse in 1966. Again, there were times in the 1970s when incumbent Democrats might seek a higher office, leaving the seat they occupied open. Such open-seat congressional elections offered some of the only opportunities for Republicans to viably compete against or even beat a Democrat.

As a political scientist, I am convinced, for the purposes of policy-making and representation, Arkansas needs two viable and competitive parties. This was true in the prior century, when primarily Democrats led the state, and it is true today. Given where the two parties are now, one might argue that today's partisan balance suggests a familiar one in Arkansas's past. The exceptions, however, are the party in power has flipped, a large segment of the voting populace appears content with one-party control, and the minority party—now, the Democratic Party—is the perennial underdog in most cases, but may, from time to time, benefit from a GOP slip or strategic error. However, things are likely worse now for Democrats today than they were for the GOP in the 1970s and 1980s. The ideological distance between the party in power and party out of power now, unlike the 1970s or 1980s, is consistently far apart. There are no moderating forces among the parties currently, and more Arkansans—at least those voting—are favoring the more conservative ideals of the GOP over the progressive messaging of the Democrats.

In order for Democrats to become a more viable party moving forward, they will likely need to review recent GOP success and accept that it did not happen overnight, but over several decades. Democrats are now at a point in the state where they must make a long-term commitment to rebuilding and cultivating a bench of political talent from which to recruit; they must focus on the organizational aspects of the party—revitalizing county committees, for example; and, last but not least, they must effectively communicate a message and brand that resonates with a larger share of Arkansas voters. These things together will not likely yield immediate results and may take years to fully bear fruit. However, by accepting their current position as the "out party" and facing hard truths about the work ahead, they can be poised to take action when the political climate becomes more favorable—much like the modern GOP in its second generation.

The purpose of this book was to provide a record of the dramatic partisan change in Arkansas. In a short period, the state went from arguably one of the most Democratic in the United States to one of the most Republican. In our polarized and fast-paced politics, it may be difficult to sit back for a moment and consider such a historical shift. However, by recognizing and exploring this sea change, you better understand the politics of the Natural State and the dynamics at play in several other states that witness partisan shifts. What happened in Arkansas was unique in its apparent suddenness and severity, but parties change, and the partisan balance in states change. This study can help explain state-level partisan change in a broader context. Nonetheless, this is a book about Arkansas, and perhaps Rex Nelson's remarks are the best to close this chapter in the state's recent political history:

> I don't care if you're Democrat, Republican, or independent. But if you love Arkansas history like we do, if you love politics, to consider the fact that ten years ago from when we're taping this—right before the election

of 2020—we had heavy Democratic majorities in both the state House and the state Senate; we had seven Democratic Constitutional officers . . . five of the six in our congressional delegation were Democrats. Here we sit, a decade later, with heavy Republican majorities: seven Republican Constitutional officers and six Republican members of the congressional delegation. The speed with which that took off, from a historic standpoint, is just absolutely breathtaking.[13]

NOTES

1. Introduction

1. Diane D. Blair and Jay Barth, *Arkansas Politics and Government*, 2nd ed. (Lincoln: University of Nebraska Press, 2005).
2. V. O. Key Jr., *Southern Politics in State and Nation* (New York: Vintage Books, 1949), 183.
3. Janine A. Parry, Andrew Dowdle, Abby Long, and Jesse Kloss, "The Rule, Not the Exception: One-Party Monopolies in the American States," *State Politics and Policy Quarterly* (forthcoming).
4. Jim Ranchino, *Faubus to Bumpers: Arkansas Votes, 1960–1970* (Arkadelphia, AR: Action Research, 1972), 90.
5. Earl Black and Merle Black, *The Rise of Southern Republicans* (Cambridge, MA: Harvard University Press, 2002).
6. Neal R. Peirce, *The Deep South States of America: People, Politics, and Power in the Seven States of the Deep South* (New York: W. W. Norton and Company, 1974); Ranchino, *Faubus to Bumpers*.
7. Morris P. Fiorina and Samuel Jeremy Abrams, "Political Polarization in the American Public," *Annual Review of Political Science* 11 (June 2008): 563–88; Seth J. Hill and Chris Tausanovitch, "Southern Realignment, Party Sorting, and the Polarization of American Primary Electorates, 1958–2012," *Public Choice* 176, no. 1/2 (July 2018): 107–32.
8. Diane D. Blair, *Arkansas Politics and Government: Do the People Rule?* (Lincoln: University of Nebraska Press, 1988).
9. Diane D. Blair, "The Big Three of Late Twentieth-Century Arkansas Politics: Dale Bumpers, Bill Clinton, and David Pryor," *Arkansas Historical Quarterly* 54, no. 1 (Spring 1995): 53–79.
10. William D. Schreckhise, Janine A. Parry, and Todd G. Shields, "Rising Republicanism in the Arkansas Electorate? A Characterization of Arkansans' Political Attitudes and Participation Rates," *Midsouth Political Science Review* 5, no. 1 (2001): 1–19; Jay Barth and Janine A. Parry, "Still Swingin': Arkansas and the 2004 Presidential Race," *American Review of Politics* 26 (2000): 133–54.
11. Black and Black, *Rise of Southern Republicans*, 285.

12. E. E. Schattschneider, *Party Government: American Government in Action* (New York: Routledge, 2003), 1.
13. V. O. Key Jr., *Politics, Parties, and Pressure Groups* (New York: Thomas Y. Crowell Co., 1964).
14. "Solid South" refers to the political tradition of solid Democratic rule in former Confederate states between the post-Reconstruction era and the late twentieth and early twenty-first centuries.
15. Dwain Hebda, "From Worst to First: Arkansas GOP Rises in Prominence Nationally," *Arkansas Money and Politics*, October 1, 2019, https://www.armoneyandpolitics.com/arkansas-gop-rises-prominence-nationally/.
16. Survey data was obtained from John H. Aldrich, Brad Gomez, and John Griffin, "State Party Organizations Study, 1999: State Party Questionnaire," Duke University, 1999; John C. Davis, "The Natural State in a Time of Change: A Survey-Based Analysis of State Party Organizations in Arkansas, 1999–2013," *Midsouth Political Science Review* 15, no. 2 (2014): 81–102.

2. The Three Generations of the GOP in Arkansas

1. V. O. Key Jr., *Southern Politics in State and Nation* (New York: Vintage Books, 1949).
2. Alexander Heard, *A Two-Party South* (Chapel Hill: University of North Carolina Press, 1952).
3. Rex Nelson, interview by author on behalf of the David and Barbara Pryor Center for Arkansas Oral and Visual History, 2020.
4. Jim Ranchino, *Faubus to Bumpers: Arkansas Votes, 1960–1972* (Arkadelphia, AR: Action Research, 1972).
5. Cathy Kunzinger Urwin, *Agenda and Reform: Winthrop Rockefeller as Governor of Arkansas 1967–1971* (Fayetteville: University of Arkansas Press, 1991); Diane D. Blair, *Arkansas Politics and Government: Do the People Rule?* (Lincoln: University of Nebraska Press, 1988).
6. John Ward, *The Arkansas Rockefeller* (Baton Rouge: Louisiana State University Press, 1978). Ward references an *Arkansas Democrat* article dated February 19, 1963.
7. Ward, *Arkansas Rockefeller*.
8. Urwin, *Agenda and Reform*.
9. Blair, *Arkansas Politics and Government*.
10. Ranchino, *Faubus to Bumpers*, 41.
11. Ranchino, *Faubus to Bumpers*, 43.
12. Urwin, *Agenda and Reform*.
13. Richard E. Yates, "Arkansas: Independent and Unpredictable," in *The Changing Politics of the South*, ed. William C. Havard (Baton Rouge: Louisiana State University Press, 1972), 293.
14. Urwin, *Agenda and Reform*.
15. Jay Barth, "Republican Party," *Encyclopedia of Arkansas* (Central Arkansas Library System, 2017), https://encyclopediaofarkansas.net/entries/republican-party-594/.
16. Donald E. Whistler, *Citizen Legislature: The Arkansas General Assembly* (Indianapolis: Western Newspaper Publishing Co., 2010).

17. Tom W. Dillard, "Winthrop Rockefeller," in *The Governors of Arkansas: Essays in Political Biography*, ed. Timothy P. Donovan, Willard B. Gatewood Jr., and Jeannie M. Whayne (Fayetteville: University of Arkansas Press, 1995), 245.
18. Ranchino, *Faubus to Bumpers*, 41.
19. Diane D. Blair, "The Big Three of Late Twentieth-Century Arkansas Politics: Dale Bumpers, Bill Clinton, and David Pryor," *Arkansas Historical Quarterly* 54, no. 1 (Spring 1995): 53–79.
20. Blair, "Big Three of Late Twentieth-Century Arkansas Politics," 65–66.
21. Blair, *Arkansas Politics and Government*, 69.
22. "1978 Arkansas Elections: A Compilation of Primary, Run-off, and General Election Results for State and District Offices," Arkansas Secretary of State, accessed June 23, 2023, https://www.sos.arkansas.gov/uploads/elections/1978%20Election%20Results.pdf.
23. Blair, *Arkansas Politics and Government*.
24. Blair, *Arkansas Politics and Government*, 67.
25. Gary D. Wekkin, "Arkansas: Electoral Competition in the 1990s," in *The New Politics of the Old South: An Introduction to Southern Politics*, ed. Charles S. Bullock III and Mark J. Rozell (Washington, DC: Rowman & Littlefield, 1998), 185–204.
26. Diane D. Blair and Robert L. Savage, "The Appearances of Realignment and Dealignment in Arkansas," in *The South's New Politics: Realignment and Dealignment*, ed. Robert H. Swansbrough and David M. Brodsky (Columbia: University of South Carolina Press, 2011), 127.
27. Arkansas voters approved a constitutional amendment in 1984 that extended the term of office for governor from two years to four years, which took effect in 1986.
28. In the 1982 election cycle, when all thirty-five Senate seats were up for grabs, the GOP filed a candidate in eleven of those races.
29. "Arkansas Election Results: 1984," Arkansas Secretary of State, accessed June 23, 2023, https://www.sos.arkansas.gov/uploads/elections/1984%20Election%20Results.pdf.
30. Ken Coon, *Heroes and Heroines of the Journey: The Builders of the Modern Republican Party of Arkansas* (self-pub., 2015), 49; Blair, *Arkansas Politics and Government*.
31. Wekkin, "Arkansas," 186.
32. Blair and Savage, "Appearances of Realignment and Dealignment in Arkansas."
33. David Maraniss, "Before Race Began, Clinton Resolved Pledge Not to Run," July 15, 1992, https://www.washingtonpost.com/archive/politics/1992/07/15/before-race-began-clinton-resolved-pledge-not-to-run/696cb650-3dab-4fcc-97dd-8bdcbb4b50f5/; Griffin Coop, "James Luin 'Skip' Rutherford III (1950–)," *Encyclopedia of Arkansas*, last updated June 16, 2023, https://encyclopediaofarkansas.net/entries/james-luin-skip-rutherford-iii-3767/.
34. Coon, *Heroes and Heroines of the Journey*.
35. "1992 Election Results," Arkansas Secretary of State, accessed June 23, 2023, https://www.sos.arkansas.gov/elections/for-election-results.
36. Wekkin, "Arkansas."
37. "No Clear Favorite in Ark. Senate Race," CNN.com, November 2, 1996, https://www.cnn.com/ALLPOLITICS/1996/news/9611/02/senate/ar/index.shtml.
38. Wekkin, "Arkansas," 187–88.

39. Andrew Dowdle and Gary D. Wekkin, "Arkansas: The Post-2000 Elections—Continued GOP Growth or a Party That Has Peaked?" in *The New Politics of the Old South: An Introduction to Southern Politics*, ed. Charles S. Bullock III and Mark J. Rozell (Washington, DC: Rowman & Littlefield, 2007), 214.
40. Winthrop Paul Rockefeller was the son of Winthrop Rockefeller, the first modern Republican to be elected governor in 1966.
41. Steve Barnes, "Arkansas Lt. Gov. Winthrop Rockefeller Dies at 57," *New York Times*, July 17, 2006, https://www.nytimes.com/2006/07/17/us/17rockefeller.html.
42. "Hutchinson Announces 2006 Gubernatorial Run," *Los Angeles Times*, March 13, 2005, https://www.nytimes.com/2006/07/17/us/17rockefeller.html.
43. Mark Carter, "Bypassing Purple: Arkansas' Switch from Blue to Red Was Quick and Definitive," *Arkansas Money and Politics*, October 2019, https://www.armoneyandpolitics.com/bypassing-purple-arkansas-switch-blue-red/.
44. Dowdle and Wekkin, "Arkansas."
45. Andrew Dowdle and Joseph D. Giammo, "Arkansas: As Red as the Rest?" in *The New Politics of the Old South: An Introduction to Southern Politics*, ed. Charles S. Bullock III and Mark J. Rozell (Washington, DC: Rowman & Littlefield, 2014), 207–18.
46. Janine A. Parry, "The Arkansas Poll, 2020: Summary Report," Fulbright College of Arts and Sciences, University of Arkansas, accessed May 24, 2023, https://fulbright.uark.edu/departments/political-science/partners/arkansas-poll.php.

3. The Changing Arkansas Electorate and the Rise of the GOP in Arkansas

1. V. O. Key Jr., *Southern Politics in State and Nation* (New York: A. A. Knopf, 1949); Janine A. Parry, Andrew Dowdle, Abby Long, and Jesse Kloss, "The Rule, Not the Exception: One-Party Monopolies in the American States," in *State Politics and Policy Quarterly* (forthcoming).
2. Boris Heersink and Jeffrey A. Jenkins, *Republican Party Politics and the American South, 1865–1968* (New York: Cambridge University Press, 2020).
3. Heersink and Jenkins, *Republican Party Politics and the American South*, 265.
4. Rex Nelson, interview conducted by author on behalf of the David and Barbara Pryor Center for Arkansas Oral and Visual History, 2020.
5. Jim Ranchino, *Faubus to Bumpers: Arkansas Votes, 1960–1972* (Arkadelphia, AR: Action Research, 1972), 9.
6. Ranchino, *Faubus to Bumpers*, 10.
7. Ranchino, *Faubus to Bumpers*, 10.
8. "Rep. Robinson Changes His Party Affiliation," C-SPAN, July 28, 1989, https://www.c-span.org/video/?8513-1/rep-robinson-party-affiliation.
9. *Arkansas Gazette*, "What Tommy Said," July 29, 1989.
10. "Tommy Franklin Robinson (1942–)," *Encyclopedia of Arkansas*, last updated March 14, 2023, https://encyclopediaofarkansas.net/entries/tommy-franklin-robinson-4648/.
11. David S. Broder, "Arkansas Governor's Race a Cat's Cradle of Loyalties," *Washington Post*, May 27, 1990.

12. John Brummett, "With Passion and Purpose," *Arkansas Democrat-Gazette*, April 24, 2018, https://www.arkansasonline.com/news/2018/apr/24/with-passion-and-purpose-20180424/.
13. Jay Barth, Diane D. Blair, and Ernie Dumas, "Arkansas," in *Southern Politics in the 1990s*, ed. Alexander P. Lamis (Baton Rouge: Louisiana State University Press, 1999), 165.
14. Asa Hutchinson, interview conducted by author on behalf of the David and Barbara Pryor Center for Arkansas Oral and Visual History, 2021.
15. Hutchinson, interview, 2021.
16. Nelson, interview, 2020.
17. Hutchinson, interview, 2021.
18. Hutchinson, interview, 2021.
19. Nelson, interview, 2020.
20. Mike Huckabee, interview conducted by author on behalf of the David and Barbara Pryor Center for Arkansas Oral and Visual History, 2021.
21. Mike Beebe, interview conducted by author on behalf of the David and Barbara Pryor Center for Arkansas Oral and Visual History, 2021.
22. Charles Babington, "Obama and His Policies Prove Toxic for Arkansas Democrats," *PBS New Hour*, January 13, 2014, https://www.pbs.org/newshour/politics/obama-policies-prove-toxic-arkansas-democrats.
23. Bill Vickery, interview conducted by author on behalf of the David and Barbara Pryor Center for Arkansas Oral and Visual History, 2021.
24. Angie Maxwell, "Why Trump Became a 'Confederate' President," *Forum* 18, no. 4 (March 2020): 493–529, https://doi.org/10.1515/for-2020-2107; Angie Maxwell and Todd Shields, *The Long Southern Strategy: How Chasing White Voters in the South Changed American Politics* (Oxford: Oxford University Press, 2019).
25. Jay Barth and Janine A. Parry, "Arkansas: Trump is a Natural for the Natural State," in *The Future Ain't What It Used to Be: The 2016 Presidential Election in the South*, eds. Scott Buchanan and Branwell DuBose Kapeluck (Fayetteville: University of Arkansas Press, 2018), 127–46.
26. Nelson, interview, 2020.
27. Maxwell and Shields, *Long Southern Strategy*.
28. Jay Barth, interview conducted by author on behalf of the David and Barbara Pryor Center for Arkansas Oral and Visual History, 2021.
29. Hutchinson, interview, 2021.
30. Hutchinson, interview, 2021.
31. Davy Carter, interview by author on behalf of the David and Barbara Pryor Center for Arkansas Oral and Visual History, 2021.
32. John Brummett, interview by author on behalf of the David and Barbara Pryor Center for Arkansas Oral and Visual History, 2021.
33. Brummett, interview, 2021.
34. Ranchino, *Faubus to Bumpers*.
35. Diane D. Blair and Jay Barth, *Arkansas Politics and Government: Do the People Rule?*, 2nd ed. (Lincoln: University of Nebraska Press, 2005); Janine A. Parry, "The Arkansas

Poll, 2020: Summary Report," Fulbright College of Arts and Sciences, University of Arkansas, accessed May 24, 2023, https://fulbright.uark.edu/departments/political-science/partners/arkansas-poll.php.

36. "Quick Facts," United States Census, accessed May 24, 2023, https://www.census.gov/quickfacts/AR.

37. Mary Hightower, "Two-Thirds of Arkansas' Counties Lost Population: What Are the Consequences?" University of Arkansas Division of Agriculture Research and Extension, May 21, 2018, https://www.uaex.uada.edu/media-resources/news/2018/may2018/05-21-2018-Ark-Population-Changes.aspx.

38. "Census Data Shows Big Growth in NW Arkansas, Dramatic Losses in Delta," *Talk Business and Politics*, February 9, 2011, https://talkbusiness.net/2011/02/census-data-shows-big-growth-in-nw-arkansas-dramatic-losses-in-delta/; Stephen Simpson, "New Census Data Raises Concern about Delta's Future Clout," August 13, 2021, https://www.arkansasonline.com/news/2021/aug/13/new-census-data-raises-concern-in-delta/.

39. Janine A. Parry and Jay Barth, "Arkansas: Another Anti-Obama Aftershock," in *Second Verse, Same as the First: The 2012 Presidential Election in the South*, ed. Scott E. Buchanan and Branwell DuBose Kapeluck (Fayetteville: University of Arkansas Press, 2014), 123–42, https://doi.org/10.2307/j.ctt1ffjhxz.14.

4. State Party Organizations and the Rise of the GOP in Arkansas

1. V. O. Key Jr., *Politics, Parties, and Pressure Groups* (New York: Thomas Y. Crowell Co., 1964).

2. Survey data was obtained from John H. Aldrich, Brad Gomez, and John Griffin, "State Party Organizations Study, 1999: State Party Questionnaire," Duke University, 1999.

3. John C. Davis and Drew Kurlowski, "Campaign Inc.: Data from a Field Survey of State Party Organizations," *Midsouth Political Science Review* 18, no. 1 (2017): 1–26.

4. V. O. Key Jr., *Southern Politics in State and Nation* (New York: A. A. Knopf, 1949); Diane D. Blair, *Arkansas Politics and Government: Do the People Rule?* (Lincoln: University of Nebraska Press, 1988).

5. Blair, *Arkansas Politics and Government*, 98–99.

6. Ken Coon, *Heroes and Heroines of the Journey: The Builders of the Modern Republican Party of Arkansas* (self-pub., 2015).

7. David A. Dulio and R. Sam Garrett, "Organizational Strength and Campaign Professionalism in State Parties," in *The State of the Parties: The Changing Role of Contemporary American Parties*, ed. John C. Green and Daniel J. Coffey, 5th ed. (Lanham, MD: Rowman & Littlefield, 2007), 199–216.

8. Cornelius Cotter, James L. Gibson, John F. Bibby, and Robert J. Huckshorn, *Party Organizations in American Politics* (New York: Praeger, 1984).

9. The state-level data from the 1984 Cotter et al. survey—available from the Interuniversity Consortium for Political Science and Social Research—has been censored for privacy issues. The author's attempts to acquire the state-identifiable results have failed.

10. On the one hand, broadening the pool of potential respondents within each organization

presents the opportunity for a higher response rate. On the other hand, expanding the potential pool of respondents beyond state party chairpersons exclusively might introduce bias when comparing the results of this survey to those of Aldrich et al. However, considering both state parties in this analysis were led by different chairpersons in 2013 than in the 1999, the potential for respondent bias could not have been avoided if Davis and Kurlowski had limited their potential pool of respondents to chairpersons. While it is possible that a party's chairperson and its executive director could give different answers to survey questions, given the objective nature of the questions posed in both surveys it is assumed that each respondent answered the questions honestly and to the best of his or her knowledge.

11. Anonymous party official quote obtained by author.
12. In 1999, the Democratic Party of Arkansas reported an election year budget of $1.5 million. The amount presented in Table 4.1 adjusts for inflation (USD 2013).
13. In 1999, the Democratic Party of Arkansas reported a nonelection-year budget of $500,000. The amount presented in Table 4.1 adjusts for inflation (USD 2013).
14. In 1999 the Republican Party of Arkansas reported an election-year budget of $1.5 million. The amount presented in Table 4.2 adjusts for inflation (USD 2013).
15. In 1999, the Republican Party of Arkansas reported a nonelection-year budget of $500,000. The amount presented in Table 4.2 adjusts for inflation (USD 2013).
16. Linda L. Fowler and Robert D. McClure, *Political Ambition: Who Decides to Run for Congress* (New Haven, CT: Yale University Press, 1990); Alan Ehrenhalt, *The United States of Ambition: Politicians, Power, and the Pursuit of Office* (New York: Times Books, 1991); Gary F. Moncrief, Peverill Squire, and Malcolm E. Jewell, *Who Runs for the Legislature?* (Upper Saddle River, NJ: Prentice Hall, 2001); Kira Sanbonmatsu, "The Legislative Party and Candidate Recruitment in the American States," *Party Politics* 12, no. 2 (2006): 233–56; James L. Gibson, Cornelius P. Cotter, John F. Bibby, and Robert J. Huckshorn, "Assessing Party Organizational Strength," *American Journal of Political Science* 27, no. 2 (May 1983): 193–222.
17. Thomas A. Kazee and Mary C. Thornberry, "Where's the Party? Congressional Candidate Recruitment and American Party Organizations," *Western Political Quarterly* 43, no. 1 (March 1990): 61–80.
18. Thomas A. Kazee and Susan L. Roberts, "Challenging a 'Safe' Incumbent: Latent Competition in North Carolina's 9th District," in *Who Runs for Congress? Ambition, Context, and Candidate Emergence*, ed. Thomas A. Kazee (Washington, DC: CQ Press, 1994), 101–18.
19. Karl Kurtz, "The Term-Limited States," National Conference of State Legislatures, February 11, 2013, http://www.ncsl.org/research/about-state-legislatures/chart-of-term-limits-states.aspx.
20. Dulio and Garrett, "Organizational Strength and Campaign Professionalism."
21. The Democratic Party of Arkansas provides a "Voter File" for candidates and county committees for a fee.
22. Cornelius Cotter and John F. Bibby, "Institutional Development of Parties and the Thesis of Party Decline," *Political Science Quarterly* 95, no. 1 (Spring 1980): 1–27; John S. Jackson III and Robert A. Hitlin, "The Nationalization of the Democratic Party," *Western Political Quarterly* 34, no. 2 (June 1981): 270–86; Robert J.

Huckshorn, Cornelius P. Cotter, John F. Bibby, and James L. Gibson, *The Social Background and Career Patterns of State Party Leaders* (unpublished manuscript, 1982), hard copy.
23. Cornelius P. Cotter, James L. Gibson, John F. Bibby, and Robert J. Huckshorn, *Party Organizations in American Politics* (Pittsburg: University of Pittsburg Press, 1984).
24. William Crotty, *Decision for the Democrats* (Baltimore: Johns Hopkins University Press, 1978).
25. Charles Longley, "Party Reform and Party Nationalization: The Case of the Democrats," in *The Party Symbol: Readings on Political Parties*, ed. William Crotty (San Francisco: W.H. Freeman and Company, 1980), 359–78.
26. Gary D. Wekkin, "National-State Relations: The Democrats' New Federal Structure," *Political Science Quarterly* 99, no. 1 (Spring 1984): 45–72; Gary D. Wekkin, "Political Parties and Intergovernmental Relations in 1984: The Consequences of Party Renewal for Territorial Constituencies," *Publius: The Journal of Federalism* 15, no. 3 (Summer 1985): 19–37; Deil S. Wright, *Understanding Intergovernmental Relations* (Monterey, CA: Brooks/Cole Publishing, 1982).
27. John F. Bibby, "Political Parties and Federalism: The Republican National Committee," *Publius* 9, no. 1 (Winter 1979): 235.
28. Bibby, "Political Parties and Federalism."
29. The 2013 responses under the category of "candidate support" are used in place of the 1999 study's measures of county support.
30. Dwaine Marvick, "Party Organizational Personnel and Electoral Democracy in Los Angeles, 1963–1972," in *The Party Symbol: Readings on Political Parties*, ed. William Crotty (San Francisco: W. H. Freeman and Company, 1980), 65.
31. John F. Bibby, "State Party Organizations: Strengthened and Adapting to Candidate-Centered Politics and Nationalization," in *The Parties Respond: Changes in American Parties and Campaigns*, ed. L. Sandy Maisel (Boulder, CO: Westview Press, 2002), 19–46; Sarah M. Morehouse and Malcolm E. Jewell, "The Future of Political Parties in the States," in *The Book of the States*, vol. 37 (Lexington, KY: The Council of State Governments, 2005).
32. Austin Ranney, "Parties in State Politics," in *Politics in the American States*, ed. Herbert Jacob and Kenneth N. Vines, 3rd ed. (Boston: Little Brown, 1976), 51–92.
33. John H. Aldrich, "Southern Parties in State and Nation," *Journal of Politics* 62, no. 3 (August 2000): 643–70.
34. Morehouse and Jewell, "The Future of Political Parties in the States."
35. John Moritz, "Records Lay Bare Debt Load of Party; State Democrats Lag in Fundraising," *Arkansas Democrat-Gazette*, August 10, 2019, https://www.arkansasonline.com/news/2019/aug/10/records-lay-bare-debt-load-of-party-201/; Hunter Field and John Moritz, "Two Hours After Filing Period Ends, Democrat Josh Mahony Drops Out of US Senate Race," *Arkansas Democrat-Gazette*, November 12, 2019, https://www.arkansasonline.com/news/2019/nov/12/josh-mahony-drops-out-us-senate-race/; Frank E. Lockwood, "State's GOP Stocks Up for '20: Republicans Raise Cash While Democrats Recruit Candidates," *Arkansas Democrat-Gazette*, July 17, 2019, https://www.arkansasonline.com/news/2019/jul/17/state-s-gop-stocks-up-for-20-20190717/.

36. Doyle Webb, interview conducted by author on behalf of the David and Barbara Pryor Center for Arkansas Oral and Visual History, 2021.
37. Mark Carter, "Bypassing Purple: Arkansas' Switch from Blue to Red Was Quick and Definitive," *Arkansas Money and Politics*, October 2, 2019, https://armoneyandpolitics.com/bypassing-purple-arkansas-switch-blue-red/.

5. State Government and the Rise of the GOP in Arkansas

1. V. O. Key Jr., *Southern Politics in State and Nation* (New York: A. A. Knopf, 1949), 184.
2. Peverill Squire and Keith E. Ham, *101 Chambers: Congress, State Legislatures, and the Future of Legislative Studies* (Columbus: Ohio State University Press, 2005).
3. "Tim Massanelli Interview," David and Barbara Pryor Center for Arkansas Oral and Visual History, University of Arkansas, Arkansas Memories Project, September 29, 2009, https://pryorcenter.uark.edu/interview.php?thisProject=Arkansas%20Memories&thisProfileURL=MASSANELLI-Tim&displayName=&thisInterviewee=433.
4. Mike Beebe, interview conducted by author on behalf of the David and Barbara Pryor Center for Arkansas Oral and Visual History, 2021.
5. In 2020, term limits were weakened considerably: instead of a lifetime ban on serving again, a legislator may serve twelve years and return after four years.
6. Davy Carter, interview conducted by author on behalf of the David and Barbara Pryor Center for Arkansas Oral and Visual History, 2021. All quotations from Carter in chapter 5 are from this interview.
7. According to Jocelyn Guyer, Naomi Shine, MaryBeth Musumeci, and Robin Rudowitz of the Kaiser Family Foundation, "Arkansas was the first state to consider mandating enrollment in Marketplace plans for adults newly eligible for Medicaid. While states have a long history of using Medicaid funds to purchase employer-based coverage for Medicaid beneficiaries, it was not until passage of the Affordable Care Act that states began to look closely and purchasing individual insurance policies with Medicaid funds. . . . At the time, it was clear that the Arkansas legislature would not approve a traditional Medicaid expansion [following a legal challenge and a court ruling that specified enrollment would be optional, rather than mandated]. . . . To move forward, the state required an alternative approach [expansion of coverage via the private option]." Jocelyn Guyer, Naomi Shine, MaryBeth Musumeci, and Robin Rudowitz, "A Look at the Private Option in Arkansas," KFF.org, August 26, 2015, https://www.kff.org/medicaid/issue-brief/a-look-at-the-private-option-in-arkansas/.
8. Michael Rowlett, "Stephens Weighing Challenge to Governor," *Arkansas Democrat-Gazette*, May 12, 2002.
9. Michael Rowlett, "Stephens Loans Panel Cash, Still Mulls Gubernatorial Bid," *Arkansas Democrat-Gazette*, September 8, 2001.
10. John Brummett, interview conducted by author on behalf of the David and Barbara Pryor Center for Arkansas Oral and Visual History, 2021.
11. Brummett, interview, 2021.
12. Beebe, interview, 2021.
13. Asa Hutchinson, interview conducted by author on behalf of the David and Barbara Pryor Center for Arkansas Oral and Visual History, 2021.
14. Hutchinson, interview, 2021.

15. Jay Barth, interview conducted by author on behalf of the David and Barbara Pryor Center for Arkansas Oral and Visual History, 2021.
16. "State Rankings," Center for Legislative Accountability, American Conservative Union, accessed May 30, 2022, http://ratings.conservative.org/states.
17. Janine A. Parry, "The Arkansas Poll, 2020: Summary Report," Fulbright College of Arts and Sciences, University of Arkansas, accessed May 24, 2023, https://fulbright.uark.edu/departments/political-science/partners/arkansas-poll.php.

6. Conclusion

1. Daniel Breen, "In Post-Trump GOP Split, Gov. Asa Hutchinson Often at Odds with His Own Party," *National Public Radio*, May 7, 2021, https://www.npr.org/2021/05/07/994812107/in-post-trump-gop-split-gov-asa-hutchinson-often-at-odds-with-his-party; Max Brantley, "Trump Rips Asa as a 'RINO stiff,'" *Arkansas Times*, July 5, 2022, https://arktimes.com/arkansas-blog/2022/07/05/trump-rips-asa-as-a-rino-stiff.
2. Hal Bass, interview by author on behalf of the David and Barbara Pryor Center for Arkansas Oral and Visual History, 2021.
3. John C. Davis, Andrew J. Dowdle, and Joseph D. Giammo, "The 2016 Elections in Arkansas: Did Playing in Hillary's 'Home Court' Make a Difference?" in *The New Politics of the Old South*, ed. Charles S. Bullock III and Mark J. Rozell, 6th ed. (Lanham, MD: Rowman & Littlefield, 2017), 242–54.
4. John C. Davis, Andrew J. Dowdle, and Joseph D. Giammo, "Arkansas: Should We Color the State Red with a Permanent Marker?" in *The New Politics of the Old South*, ed. Charles S. Bullock III and Mark J. Rozell, 7th ed. (Lanham, MD: Rowman & Littlefield, 2021), 289–302.
5. According to the 2020 Arkansas Poll, Arkansans approval of President Trump was 58 percent, with 63 percent of "very likely voters" approving. Janine A. Parry, "The Arkansas Poll, 2020: Summary Report," Fulbright College of Arts and Sciences, University of Arkansas, accessed May 24, 2023, https://fulbright.uark.edu/departments/political-science/partners/arkansas-poll.php.
6. Tim Griffin, interview by author on behalf of the David and Barbara Pryor Center for Arkansas Oral and Visual History, 2020.
7. Andrew DeMillo, "Nationalizing Her Governor Run? 'You Bet I Am,' Sanders Says," *AP News*, September 25, 2021, https://apnews.com/article/business-arkansas-race-and-ethnicity-election-2020-little-rock-510eba764a340c9d316969aca9f494b7.
8. Angie Maxwell, interview by author on behalf of the David and Barbara Pryor Center for Arkansas Oral and Visual History, 2021.
9. Rex Nelson, interview by author on behalf of the David and Barbara Pryor Center for Arkansas Oral and Visual History, 2020.
10. Janine A. Parry, interview by author on behalf of the David and Barbara Pryor Center for Arkansas Oral and Visual History, 2021.
11. Parry, interview, 2021
12. Mike Beebe, interview by author on behalf of the David and Barbara Pryor Center for Arkansas Oral and Visual History, 2021.
13. Nelson, interview, 2020.

INDEX

Page numbers with *t* refer to tables.

Abrams, Stacey, 111
Affordable Care Act (ACA), 48–55, 88–90, 93–94
African American voters, 13, 14, 59; and biracial coalition, 36–37
Aldrich, Gomez, and Griffin study ("State Party Organizations Study"), 62, 66t, 68t; methods, 64, 71
American Conservative Union (ACU), 97–98
Arkansas Industrial Development Commission, 12, 19
Atwater, Lee, 40
Barth, Jay, 51, 96, 107–8
Bass, Hal, 104
Bearden, Richard, 46
Beebe, Mike: on bipartisanship, 94; and Democrats in state power, 30; on future of Republican and Democratic parties, 111–12; on Huckabee's appointments as governor, 47; on primary elections, 45; and Republican General Assembly, 31–32, 88, 89–90; on term limits, 86
Berry, Marion, 32
Bethune, Ed, 18, 20
Biden, Joe, 106
Big Three: Democratic Party stronghold at top of ticket, 17–18; emergence of, 5, 17; national Democratic Party's liberal stances, distancing selves from, 17–18, 23, 26, 42–43, 102. *See also* Bumpers, Dale; Clinton, Bill; Pryor, David

biracial coalition, 36–37. *See also* Rockefeller, Winthrop
Boozman, John, 32, 46, 52–53
Brandon, Doug, 18
Britt, Maurice "Footsie," 14
Broadway, Shane, 54
Brock, Roby, 48
Brummett, John, 41, 54–55, 92–93
Bryant, Winston, 27
Bumpers, Dale, 15, 26, 37, 42. *See also* Big Three
Bush, George H. W., 25, 39
Bush, George W., 28, 31, 52
candidate recruitment, 28, 47–48, 69–71, 108–9, 113
Carter, Davy, 53, 87–90, 92–94
Carter, Jimmy, 39
Causey, Chad, 32
Center for Legislative Accountability (CLA), 97–98
Civil Rights Act (1964), 13, 36, 50
Clinton, Bill: congressional campaign, 16; gubernatorial campaigns, 19–20, 21–22, 39–42; national Democratic Party, distancing self from liberal policies of, 39, 42–43; national prominence, rise of, 21–22; presidency and power vacuum in state, 25, 32–33, 44, 102–3; as president, 52; presidential campaign, 25, 39–40; and Rockefeller's legacy, 37. *See also* Big Three
Clinton, Hillary, 50, 104

Congressional District, Second, 18, 21, 32, 40
Congressional District, Third, 32. *See also* Hammerschmidt, John Paul
Congressional District, Fourth, 25
conservatism, 95–99, 103–5, 106, 113
county committees, 78, 94, 113
Crank, Marian, 37
Crawford, Rick, 32
Darr, Mark, 54
Davis and Kurlowski study ("Campaign Inc."), 62, 66t, 68t; methods, 64, 71
Democratic Party, national: branding, 90; civil rights and social liberalization, 17–18, 23, 38–42, 50, 54–55; Democratic National Convention and Bill Clinton, 39; and Democratic Party of Arkansas, coordination, 65, 72–73, 73t. *See also* nationalization of state politics
Democratic Party of Arkansas: and campaign issue development, 71; and candidate recruitment and support, 70, 70t, 71–72, 72t; institutional characteristics, 64–67, 66t, 69; and national Democratic Party, coordination, 65, 72–73, 73t; and national Democratic Party, distancing from, 54–55 (*see also* Big Three); party organizational strength, 62, 75–77, 79, 91, 113
Dickey, Betty, 46
Dickey, Jay, 25, 29
Dulio and Garrett study: methods, 75
election cycle of 1964, 11, 13–14, 32
election cycle of 1966, 11, 14, 16, 23, 32, 37–38
election cycle of 1968, 11, 15, 17, 23, 38
election cycle of 1970, 11, 16, 17
election cycle of 1972, 17, 18
election cycle of 1974, 16
election cycle of 1978, 19
election cycle of 1980, 19–20
election cycle of 1990, 21–22, 24–25, 39–42
election cycle of 1992, 25, 85, 102
election cycle of 1996, 26–27
election cycle of 2000, 29
election cycle of 2002, 29
election cycle of 2006, 29–30
election cycle of 2008, 30
election cycle of 2010, 31, 52–53, 87
election cycle of 2012, 87–88
election cycle of 2020, 104
Elliott, Joyce, 32
Faubus, Orval, 12–14, 37
Fulbright, J. William, 23, 38
General Assembly: conservative ranking of, 97–98, 97t; political makeup in third generation, 83, 84t, 87–90
generations, periodization and characteristics: first generation, 11–24, 32–33, 85, 102; second generation, 24–30, 85, 102–3; third generation, 31–32, 33–34, 103
Goldwater, Barry, 13
governor, appointment power of, 27, 46–48
Griffin, Tim, 32, 106
Hammerschmidt, John Paul, 11, 14, 16, 24, 25, 32, 38
Hispanic population, 109
Huckabee, Mike: building of Republican Party, 27–28, 46–48; governor, ascension to, 3, 33, 44; as governor, tenure of, 29, 46–48; lieutenant governor, special election to, 26; threat of primary challenger, 91–92
Hutchinson, Asa: and bipartisanship, 92–93; building Republican Party, 105; as chair of Arkansas Republican Party, 24–25, 63; on Clinton's presidential election and effects, 44; on conservatism, 95–96; criticism that RINO, 103; as governor, 90; gubernatorial election, 29–30; and intraparty conflicts, 94–95; on Lincoln and Boozman, 52–53; on Obama, 52; and primary elections, changes to, 44–45; on ticket-splitting, 43–44; US House, election to, 27
Hutchinson, Tim, 5, 25, 27, 29–30
income tax, 95
independent voters: increasing identification of, 21; Republican leaning, shift to, 55–58
interviewees, list of, 8t

Johnson, Jim, 14, 37
Key, V. O., Jr., 2, 77, 81–82
Lincoln, Blanche Lambert, 32, 46, 49, 52–53
Massanelli, Tim, 85–86
Maxwell, Angie, 108–9
McRae, Tom, IV, 41–42
media, 48–49, 52, 54, 93
Medicaid, 96
Medicare, 93–94
Moore, Robert, 87–88
National Governors Association, 39
nationalization of state politics, 48–55, 99, 102, 105–6, 110
Nelson, Rex: on Clinton's presidential elections and effects, 44; on future of Republican Party of Arkansas, 109; on Huckabee organization, 46; on Obama and race, 50; on Rockefeller, 12, 37; on speed of political shift, 113–14
Nelson, Sheffield, 21–22, 24–25, 40–42, 63
Nixon, Richard, 18, 39
Northwest Arkansas, 2, 12, 25, 30, 36, 58–60, 109, 111. *See also* Hammerschmidt, John Paul
Obama, Barack, 48–55, 78, 88–90
Obamacare. *See* Affordable Care Act (ACA)
one-party dominance: candidates, quality of, 107–8; challenges of, 103–5; and intraparty conflict, 77, 90–95, 98–99; and party strength, 79, 81–83
open seats, effects of in election, 85, 86–87, 112
Parry, Janine A., 109–11
party affiliation, 38–39, 41, 45–46, 48, 55–58, 56t, 57t, 99. *See also* ticket-splitting
polarization in politics, 91–96, 113
political parties, role of, 5–6; two-party system as necessary for democracy, 12–13, 77, 112
population demographics, 58–60; Hispanic population, 109; urban versus rural, 110–11
populist appeal, 104–5. *See also* Robinson, Tommy; Wallace, George

Post Office Republicans, 12
primary elections: against incumbents, 91–95; legal challenge to, 44–45; open partisan, 41; primary challengers, role of, 91–95; role of, 38
projections for future, 58–60, 107–14
Pryor, David, 20, 26, 37, 42, 119. *See also* Big Three
Pryor, Mark, 29–30, 31, 46, 49
Reagan, Ronald, 19, 39
redistricting, 59, 108
Republican Party, national: branding, 90, 105–6; and Republican Party of Arkansas, coordination, 72–73, 74, 74t, 99. *See also* nationalization of state politics
Republican Party of Arkansas: branding, 78, 97–99; and campaign issue development, 71; and candidate recruitment and support, 70, 71–72, 71t, 72t; institutional characteristics, 67–69, 68t, 78–79; intraparty conflicts and conservatism, 13, 15, 19, 37, 91–95; and national Republican Party, coordination, 72–73, 74, 74t, 99; party organizational strength, 46–48, 62, 75–79
Republican Party of Arkansas v. Faulkner County Arkansas, 45
RINOs (Republicans in name only), 103
Robinson, Tommy, 21–22, 24, 40–42, 105
Rockefeller, Nelson, 13
Rockefeller, Winthrop: coalition of voters, 15, 19, 23, 36–37, 39, 82, 102; and Democratic General Assembly, 14–15; first generation, beginning of, 2, 11, 32; gubernatorial campaigns, 13–14; Republican Party rebuilding, limited success of, 12–13, 15–17, 82–83; on two-party system, need for, 12–13
Rockefeller, Winthrop Paul, 29–30
Ross, Mike, 29, 31–32
Rutherford, Skip, 41
Sanders, Sarah Huckabee, 106, 109–10
Snyder, Vic, 32
Solid South: definition of, 116n14

Southern Strategy, 50, 108
speaker of the Arkansas House of
    Representatives. *See* Carter, Davy
Tea Party movement, 51, 78
term limits, 21, 70, 76, 83–87
Thornton v. United States, 85
ticket-splitting, 17–18, 29, 43–44, 99, 102, 106
Trump, Donald, 103, 104–5, 110, 111–12
Tucker, Jim Guy, 3, 18, 26, 33, 44
Vickery, Bill, 48–49, 87
Voting Rights Act (1965), 50
Wallace, George, 17, 23, 38, 50, 105
Webb, Doyle, 7, 30, 77, 78, 103
White, Frank, 2
white rural voters, 51, 59–60, 106
Whitewater investigation, 26
Womack, Steve, 32

About the Author

John C. Davis is the executive director of the David and Barbara Pryor Center for Arkansas Oral and Visual History and associate teaching professor of political science at the University of Arkansas. An eighth-generation Arkansan, Davis lives with his family in Fayetteville.